Beowulf

TRANSLATED INTO VERSE BY

WILLIAM ELLERY LEONARD

AND ILLUSTRATED BY

LYND WARD

FOR THE MEMBERS OF THE HERITAGE CLUB

NEW YORK

Something About the Poem Beowulf

THE story of Beowulf, the Strong Man and the Helper of Man-kind, comes from pretty far away and pretty long ago. It was a story that grew up across the seas in the fjords of Western Scandinavia and the marshy coasts and low plains of Denmark, in the times when the chiefs and their retainers in their halls and the farmer-folk in their homesteads, during the long winter evenings of the north, used to enjoy make-believe and song of the harp. It was really a collection of stories, some of them historical traditions of Viking voyages and real battles, but most of them stories invented by the folk-imagination, like Jack the Giant Killer and other fairy stories about strange and tremendous adventures. But they were invented in such a lively manner that doubtless both the tellers and the listeners came to half-believe them true—just as every child half-believes the story of Jack the Giant Killer to be true.

And they were told over many times by many different story-tellers; and presumably almost every new story-teller added something new and interesting of his own invention. The same thing happens around the fires and in the shacks of our own lumber-camps, when the lumber-jacks tell year after year about a gigantic strong man, like Beowulf, whom they call Paul Bunyan. And when some of these folks from Scandinavia and from Denmark and from the flat country on the coast south of Denmark sailed in their crowded boats to the island of Britain, they brought along these stories—along with their swords and shields and cattle and language and wooden images of their gods. And the stories continued to grow in the new island home.

Then sometime about seven hundred and fifty, a period of some prosperity and culture, when the descendants of these old Germanic invaders and settlers had established walled towns and green homesteads, and built bridges and churches and monasteries and schools, some nameless poet took these stories (perhaps preserved in ballads) and made them into a long, stirring poem. He was not a heathen, unlettered man; but a man who knew the Bible and perhaps some Latin books like Vergil. Yet he loved the old stories of the days when his ancestors were heathen and ignorant of books, and he loved them so much and he told them so well that he ought to have left out the Bible references and the Christian piety.

And the poet of the Beowulf-stories was a man rather clever in putting different stories together as one larger story, clever too in telling about one thing in a way to make us all ears to hear about the next thing, and somehow his imagination and music puts us into a long peculiar mood and makes us feel as if we were in strange, mysterious realms, half hidden in mist and echoing the sounds of gray, cold seas, in spite of the golden hall of Heorot and the flashing of brave men's helmets and swords. His art has a massive, weird vagueness. It is a very different art from that of the story-tellers of old Iceland. In the younger Edda, for instance, we read that once "Thor grasped his hammer-handle so hard that *his knuckles grew white.*" Homely, realistic details like this are not in our poet's manner at all. There is a world of difference between strange shadowy shapes and familiar vivid outlines; but each of the two worlds of art has its own peculiar meaning and suggestion for our imagination. And our poet has the old-time warrior's love of battle. A terrible love was that— not ignoble, but terrible—when we think what it has always meant in blood and pain and tears. What a piece of work is man, after all, that so much of his great loyalty and great honor and valor should have been spent then, and spent ever since, on killing. But in the poem *Beowulf*, the foes that are killed are chiefly Ogres and Dragons —real enemies of civilization and human happiness (not merely members of other tribes like ourselves whom our hatred and fear distorts into Monsters). That is why I for one can rejoice in most of Beowulf's battle-work, though I am a pacifist and what Theodore Roosevelt used to call a molly-coddle.

IV

The poet of *Beowulf* was also a man clever in making verses—in those days a very special craft. There were not all kinds of metres as nowadays; there was just one. This had been developed and handed down by poets long, long before the poet who used it in telling the Beowulf-stories. There was for many generations this one way of making verses, as there was for long years one way of making shields out of linden-wood or of weaving cloth for dress. For in old times there was less change and variety in the way folks made things. The father taught his son, the mother her daughter, and the master his apprentice the old devices and methods in every art and custom. So our poet had learned an art, a special kind of verse-craft, handed down from the past.

Perhaps the reader would like to see a sample of that old verse. Here are two lines:

> Gewát tha òfer *w*áeg-hòlm, *w*índè gefýsèd,
> Flótà *f*ámi-héals *f*úglà gelícòst

They mean:

"Then went over the billowy ocean, driven by the wind, the floater (ship), with foamy neck (prow), very like a (wild-) fowl."

Now, if he'll pardon a somewhat twisted translation, I can put these verses into a sort of equivalent English verse. Like this:

> Wént she òver *w*áve-sèas, *w*índỳ her fáring,
> Flóatèr *f*óamy-nécked— *f*ówl wàs she líkèst.

The observant student will notice: (1) that the lines are divided by a pause in the middle; and (2) that the two halves of each line have words that begin with the same sound (alliteration).

He will notice, too, the accent-marks over some of the syllables both in the Anglo-Saxon and the English. I just now set them there to help explain the way the verses keep time. In the old days verses were not read to one's self, or even read aloud or recited; they were sung, or half-sung, or chanted, to the accompaniment of the harp, before a group of listeners at festivals, feasts, or parties. So they kept time in a very marked degree. There were four beats to each half-line. Some were very strong beats, especially those beats that fell on the alliterating syllables. These I mark with a stroke like this: ´. Some were quite weak—little beats made clear by being accompanied by little pauses. These I mark with a stroke like this: `. But *the time was marked* just as definitely by the light beats as by the heavy ones. There is nothing mysterious about it. When one chants

> Sing a sóng of síx-pènce   a bág fùll of rýe,
> Fóur and twénty bláckbìrds   báked ìn a píe,

he marks time by both strong and weak beats—strong on 'bag' and on 'baked,' and weak on 'full' and on 'in.' The student will notice, again, that sometimes two accents come next to each other without any unaccented syllable between; that was a characteristic trick in Anglo-Saxon verse, a trick sometimes made use of in the kind of modern English verse that has carried on the old traditional way of verse-making.

Now in my translation of the whole poem of *Beowulf* I've used a verse-form like that of "Sing a song of sixpence," a form which really developed out of this same old Anglo-Saxon verse. I am really concerned that the reader get the music, the beats, of this verse of mine. I think he will, by just chanting, or half-chanting, it aloud. Let him read these lines aloud:

> Thèn aròund the móund ròde   with crý ànd cáll [páuse]
> Báirns òf the *áe*thelìngs   twélve òf áll [páuse],
> To *móurn* fòr their Mástèr   their sórròw to síng [páuse],
> Frámìng a wórd-chànt,   spéaking òf the Kíng [páuse].

He will notice: (1) that there is a pause in the middle of each line, as in the Anglo-Saxon; (2) that there are many syllables beginning with the same sound, as in the Anglo-Saxon, but that they are not arranged with the same uniformity of number and position; (3) that there are combinations of heavy beats (´) and light beats (`) as in the Anglo-Saxon; and (4) that sometimes two accented syllables come

VI

together with no unaccented syllable between, just as in the Anglo-Saxon too. But on the other hand he will notice that my verses rhyme (usually, as in this sample, in rhyme-*pairs*). And he will notice that, though in each first half-line there are four beats as in the old verse, there *seem* to be only three beats on each second half-line. I say "*seem* to be"; because there is, as one chants the lines, a natural pause always *of the same length* after each rhyme; and a boy, beating time with a stick or his finger, would make one beat there in the air between the end of one line and the beginning of the next. So, though my line has only seven beats on the words, it really has eight beats as *music,* like the Anglo-Saxon, if one counts, as one should, the end-pause, or rest. (The pause in the middle is shorter, the time being kept by the light beat plus the short pause.)

But how is it that this old poem in a dead language has been preserved for us, so that I or any other man could read it and translate? The Beowulf-stories were originally handed down by word of mouth, in the same way as the stories, the legends and myths, of the American Indians. I think myself that the poet who wove those stories together himself wrote out his poem; even though he delivered it from memory, chanting it to his harp. Anyway, some one wrote it down and others afterwards copied it. They probably copied it in the monasteries, for the monks were about the only men who were handy with the pen, and they probably made the copies for pay "to fill orders" from wealthy burghers or noblemen who could afford the luxury of books, so long before the days of printing.

One copy only has come down to us. It is on parchment, and, from the kind of handwriting and from the kind of spelling, scholars judge it must have been made about the year 1000—that is, about one hundred years after the death of King Alfred, or two hundred and fifty years after the poem itself was composed. It was discovered over two hundred years ago, and is now preserved in the British Museum at London. Two scribes made it. The first wrote in a finer, the second in a much coarser hand. And the second took up the task just before the end of a sentence (and of a verse). This makes me

VII

wonder if the first scribe suddenly went blind or took sick or died right there at his desk. Otherwise, we would have to believe the scribes worked in a very mechanical way, with even less interest in the subject matter than my stenographer who typed this translation of mine for the printer.

And the ink is faded, and the parchment is charred by the heat from a fire in an old library where it used to be kept. So it's not always easy to make out the words. Thus it is that many scholars of England, America, Germany, and the Scandinavian countries, with microscope and pen and paper and grammar and dictionary, have studied it and copied it, filling in by shrewd guesses missing letters or words, and sometimes even changing letters, when by the change they thought they could improve the sense. And they have published their revised and corrected texts with many explanatory notes; and their difficult labors have given us what we call "editions of *Beowulf*." There are many, I say. The last edition is that of Professor F. Klaeber at the University of Minnesota, but it was published (Heath and Co.) only after my version was completed. The next to the last is that of R. W. Chambers. This is not the American R. W. Chambers whose novels one's suburban aunt is so fond of. This R. W. C. is a scholar at University College, London. I have translated from his text of the poem (Cambridge University Press, 1914); but now and then I have adopted the words with which some other editors have patched up the ragged spots. And I haven't bothered to ask anybody's permission, nor said anything about it in footnotes. Thus the sympathetic reader may be sure some reviewer will call me "unscholarly." I won't mind, so long as I help fireside lovers of Hector and Achilles and Odysseus to love too my old Germanic hero of the mighty grip—and so long as the teachers' conventions recommend my little book for colleges and schools.

If one wants to follow up the subject of *Beowulf*—wants to know more about this old poetry and these old legends—I suggest he look sometime at the following books:

Chambers' *Introduction to Beowulf*,

Olrik's *The Heroic Legends of Denmark* (translated from the Danish by my friend L. M. Hollander),

Gummere's *The Oldest English Epic,*

Stjerna's *Essays on Questions Connected . . . with Beowulf* (translated from the Swedish by J. R. C. Hall).

And that he may understand my ideas about Anglo-Saxon versification, let him read my two monographs, published in "The University of Wisconsin Studies in Language and Literature":

Beowulf and the Niebelungen Couplet,

The Scansion of Middle English Alliterative Verse.

For information on the old life and customs around the North Sea, let him read Williams' *Social Scandinavia in the Viking Age.*

Beowulf

Beowulf

THE OPENING

BEFORE *chanting the deeds of the Geatman Beowulf, so brave and so strong,*
the 'Scop' (that is, the bard) chants the story of the ancestry of Hrothgar, the
King of Danishmen (whose grandfather happened to be called Beowulf also),
especially the strange story of the coming and the burial of Scyld, founder of the
royal line. But why should the story of Beowulf, the Geat, begin with Hrothgar,
the Dane? The Scop will strike his harp again and again and make all clear.

WHAT ho! We've heard the glory   of Spear-Danes, clansmen-kings,
　　　Their deeds of olden story,—   how fought the aethelings!
Often Scyld Scefing   reft his foemen all,
Reft the tribes at wassail   of bench and mead in hall.
Smote the jarls with terror;   gat good recompense
For that he came a foundling,   a child with no defense:
He waxed beneath the welkin,   grew in honors great,
Till each and every people,   of those around who sate
Off beyond the whale-road,   to him was underling,

Beowulf

To him must tender toll-fee.   That was a goodly King!
   Unto him thereafter,   was an heir y-born,
Within his gates a youngling,   whom God that folk forlorn
For recompense was sending.   He marked the grievous wrong,
How they of old had suffered,   without a prince so long.
And so the Wonder-Wielder,   the Lord of Life, fulfilled
For them world's weal and honor,   through him, the heir of Scyld.
For famous was this Beowulf,   and far and wide there came
O'er the lands of Scandia   the vaunting of his name.
So shall youth achieve it,   with good works before,
With bold gifts and largesse,   from his father's store,
That in old age after,   when the wars may come,
Willing comrades, liegemen loyal,   may stand by at home.
Praiseful deed will bring good speed   in what clan soe'er.
   Then did Scyld betake him,   when his hour was there,
The stout and staunch betook himself   to his Lord's good care.
Then away they bore him   to the sea-tides,—did,
They, his loving clansmen,   as himself had bid,
Whilst he wielded speech-craft,   he, the Scyldings' friend,
Prince so long who ruled them,   dear to the end.
There in haven stood she,   her prow a rounded ring,
Icy and out-bound,   barge of the Aetheling.
Laid they then the dear Chief,   Bracelet-Breaker of old,
Mighty King, by the mast there,   within the good ship's hold.
And full many a treasure,   many a shining thing,
They fetched from ways afar off,   for his journeying.
Never heard I tell of   keel more fairly dight
With the warrior-weapons   and the weeds of fight,
With the blades and byrnies.   On his bosom lay
Treasure to fare with him   far o'er floods away.
Methinks not less a lading   of lordly gifts they gave
Than those who sent him whilom   a lone babe o'er the wave.

2

Beowulf

O'er his head they set, too,   golden banner steep,
Let the billows bear him,   gave him to the deep.
Theirs were souls of sorrow,   theirs were hearts to weep.
And no man can say sooth,—   none in halls of state,
None of battle-bold ones,—   who took up that freight.

I

HROTHGAR, *grown to rule powerfully over wide regions, had his people build splendid hall which he named Heorot, or, in our speech today 'Hart,' that is, 'tag,' perhaps from antlers adorning the gables (though the Scop does n't say). Here with his retainers he feasted in joy, but Grendel, a sullen and violent annibal Monster, who haunted the swamps and moors and prowled on the out-irts of the dwellings of men by night, was not pleased with the revel. What id Grendel, the Man-Eater, do?*

RULED Beowulf, the Scylding,   in burg for many a year,
Famed among the people,   a folk-king dear
(His father was ta'en elsewhere,   that chief from home was ta'en),
Until for him there woke a son,   the high Halfdane.
And Halfdane, named the Agéd   and the Fierce-in-fray,
O'er the gracious Scyldings held,   all his life, the sway.
And, lo, for him four children   (to count them as they be)
Awoke unto the world's light: warrior-leaders three,

Beowulf

Heorogar, and Hrothgar,   and Halga, named the good;
And daughter, queen (says story)   in Sweden o'er the flood.
    Now was there given to Hrothgar   such valor in the van,
Such honor in the onset,   that all his kin-of-clan
Eagerly obeyed him,   till waxed around his throne
Host of comrade-tribesmen,   warrior-youths well-grown.
It came into his mood then   to bid his serfs up-raise
A hall-chamber, a mead-house,   a mightier far for praise
Than sons of men e'er heard of,   and then within the hall
Unto young and unto old   to deal his treasures all,
Such as God had lent him,   except men's lives and lands.
To many tribes (I've heard too)   he gave his wide commands
Around this earth to deck it,   this folkstead, with their hands.
Nor was it long thereafter,   men saw its finished frame,
The greatest of hall-houses: Heorot was the name
That he whose word was mighty   had fashioned for the same.
He failed not of his vaunting,   he dealt the rings thereby,
The treasure at carousal.   Heorot towered high,
With stag-horn on each gable . . . waiting its fiery fate,
The burning after battle;   nor far the day when hate,
After old feuds, should waken,   once more betwixt the twain—
Betwixt the daughter's father   and him her wedded thane.
But now that bold Hobgoblin,   who dwelt in fenways dark,
Ill bore the sullen grievance   that he each day must hark
To revel loud at banquet.   The noise of harp was there,
In hall clear song of singer.   He spake who knew full fair
To tell mankind's beginning,   how God Almighty wrought
The earth, that shining lea-land,   which waters fold about;
Quoth how God set, triumphant,   the sun and the moon
As lights to lighten landsfolk;   how he adornéd soon
With leaf and limb the fold all;   and eke created birth
For every kind that moveth   on ocean, air, or earth.

4

Beowulf

So lived the troop of tribesmen,   in revel, wise and well,
Till One began to do misdeed—   this selfsame Fiend of hell.
And that grim Hobgoblin   was Grendel named by men,
Great Stalker of the marches,   who held the moor and fen;
Housed with the brood of giants   this joyless Wight the while,
After Lord Creator   had doomed his damned exile.
(Upon Cain's kin the Eternal   avengéd Abel's blood.
Cain gat no mirth from murder;   God banished him from good,
Afar from man, for sin's sake.   Thence woke the monster-brood,
Ettins, elves, and ogres,   and giants, too, that warred
So long with God, who paid them   at last their fit reward.)

II

The Scop *chants what it was that Grendel did. Grendel visited Heorot as the retainers slept, and seized thirty of them and made off; and there was great woe and terror at Heorot and in the Burg (town) of Danishmen. And for twelve years Grendel continued his visits, and Hrothgar and his councillors were at their wits' ends. The Scop does not say how often Grendel came or whether he always was lucky enough to make off with thirty, as on the first night; but we believe there must have been many, many Danishmen to have kept Grendel busy so long at Heorot, and it seems strange that their combined strength,—they were men, too, with such goodly spears and swords,—was not equal to slaying Cannibal Grendel. But so it was. Perhaps he bore a charmed life, and could be conquered only by Some One against whom the charm was powerless. Who might that Some One be?*

THEN fared he forth, did Grendel,   to seek at dead of night
The high house, how the Ring-Danes,   after their beer, were dight.
The aethelings he found there,   aslumber after mirth;
Naught they knew of sorrow,   naught of human dearth.
The Creature of damnation,   the grim, the greedy One,
The fierce One in his fury,   was ready there anon;
And, where they rested, reft he   thirty, thane by thane,
And thence went faring homeward,   of his plunder fain,
With his fill of slaughter,   to seek his lairs again.

   In the dawning, at the daybreak,   arose of men the wail,
A mickle morning-uproar,   after their yester-ale,
When Grendel's strength in battle   to sons of men was plain.
Blitheless sate the high Prince,   the Aetheling so good;
That strong Heart stricken sate,   o'er lost thanes abroad,
What time the court set eyes on   the curséd Monster's trail,—
Too strong that strife for Danefolk,   too long the bane and bale.

   Eftsoons, but one night after,   was he at work once more,
With more of loathly slaughter,   nor mourned a whit therefor,
A whit for feud and foul deed—   in sin was he so bound!
Then might ye mark full many   who somewhat further found
Resting-places elsewhere,—   in outer bowers their bed,
When, by so clear a token,   to them was soothly said
The hate of this new Hall-Thane.   More far, more tight, all such
Did keep themselves thereafter   who 'scaped that devil's clutch!
So ruled he and so ravaged,   in wrong the one 'gainst all,
Till idle stood and empty   that excelling hall.
Mickle long the while was: twelve winters' tide
Hrothgar dreed disaster,   woes with never end,
Sorrows unbounded,   he, the Scyldings' Friend.

Beowulf

And the mournful tidings   to courts and kingdoms wide
In gleemen's ballads travelled,   how Grendel's hate defied
Hrothgar forever,   how for many a year
Grendel waged his warfare,   strife of ceaseless fear;
Would not, by a peace-pact,   set the Danemen free,
Would not with the Aethelings   e'er compound for fee.
And still less might any   of the Wise-men wot,
'Gainst those paws of pillage,   help for Hrothgar's lot.
The grisly Wretch kept reaving   youth and age of breath;
He lurked, he lured them darkly,   that skulking Shade of Death;
Made, through nights eternal,   misty moors his home;
Though beyond man's ken the haunts,   where Hell's wizards roam.
Such a tale of terrors,   such heap of hard despite
Wrought this Foe of mankind,   Stalker lone by night.
Heorot Hall, the gold-bright,   was his dusky den.
(Yet not his the power—   God forbade him then!—
E'er to greet the gift-stool,   e'er to come anear
Throne itself of Hrothgar,   nor partake its cheer.)
And so soul of Hrothgar,   Scylding good and great,
Long was wracked and broken.   And chiefs together sate
Oft at rede, devising,   what to do were best,
For such stout-hearted clansmen,   against such awful guest.

   Whiles at their idol-temples   they vowed their offerings fair,
And conjured the Soul-Destroyer,   for help in folk-despair.
Such was their devil-practice,   and hope of these heathen men,
'Twas Hell in their hearts they remembered;   and God was not in their ken.
The Doomsman of Deeds, they wist not;   wist not the Lord of Love;
Nor worshipped the Wielder-of-Wonders,   the Helm of the Heavens above.
Woe to the soul that perversely   shall fling to the fiery pit,
Never to ween of comfort,   never to change a whit;
Weal to the soul that after   the day of his death is come
May seek the Lord and crave there   in arms of the Father a home.

Beowulf

III

*Off in Geatland, across the narrow seas in Southern Scandinavia, Beowu[lf]
the Kinsman of Hygelac, King of the Geats, heard through mariners, or throu[gh]
wandering gleemen singing of Cannibal Grendel and Heorot the Desolate, ho[w]
terrible was Hrothgar's need and distress; and he sailed forth with a chosen ban[d]
of fourteen stalwart young braves to render Hrothgar the help of his gre[at]
strength. For, as everybody knew who listened to the Scop in those days, Beo[?]
wulf was the strongest man that ever lived and the most ready to use his streng[th]
for the good of mankind. But when they landed on the Danish Shore, the Coa[st]
Guard challenged them, fearing they were spies and enemies.*

AND so the son of Halfdane   was carked by cares which bide,
     Nor might the brave and wise One   the sorrow turn aside:
Too big the strife for Danefolk,   too long the bale and bane,
This hugest of night-horrors,   that on his people came.
Far in his home, that good man,   among the Geatish breeds,
Hyglac's thane and nephew,   got word of Grendel's deeds.
Of all mankind the strongest   in might and main was he,
In the days of this our life here,   high-born and free.
Bade make ready for him   a rider-of-the-sea;
Quoth, he'd seek this War-King,   o'er the swan-road, he!—
Seek this noble Chieftain,   'for that 't is men he needs.'
The canny carls did chide him   (though he to them was dear)
Little for his faring;   nay, rather spake him cheer,
Him the battle-brave One,   and looked for omens clear.
The Good One of the Geatfolk   now picked his comrades keen:
When he sought his timbered vessel,   he was one of bold fifteen;
And well he kenned the coast-marks,   wise in sailor-craft.
    The boat ere long they launchéd,   under the bluffs abaft;
The ready warriors clambered   over the wave-tossed side;
Against the sands the breakers   were writhing with the tide;

Beowulf

On the breast of the bark the heroes   bore their bright array,
Their battle-gear so gorgeous.   They pushed the bark away,
Away on its eager voyage.   The well-braced floater flew,
The foamy-necked, the bird-like,   before the winds that blew,
Over the waves of the waters—   till, after the risen sun
Of the next day, the curved prow   her course so well had run
That these faring-men the land saw,   the cliffs aglow o'er the deep,
Broad sea promontories,   high hills steep.
Ocean now was o'er-wandered,   now was their voyaging o'er.
Thence clomb the Weder-clansmen   speedily up on the shore;
Anchored well their sea-wood,   whilst their armor clanked,
Their mailéd sarks of battle;   God Almighty thanked
Because for them the sea-paths   had not been made too hard.

    Then from the wall the Watchman,   the Scylding set to guard
The water-cliffs, espied them   over the gangway bear
Their glittering shields of linden,   their ready fighting-gear.
His wits were seized with wonder,   what men were these indeed!
Down to the strand he gat him,   riding on a steed;
Henchman, he, of Hrothgar,—   mightily did shake
With his hands his spear-shaft,   and in parley spake:
"What are ye, ye mail-clad,   what armor-bearing braves,
Who lead a keel so high-prowed   hither o'er the waves,
O'er the ocean causeway?   I've been out-post long,
Long I've held the sea-watch,   lest a pirate throng
In their fleet might sometime   do our Daneland wrong.
Here have strangers never   made them more at home;
Yet to you no word-of-leave   from my kin hath come,
No consent from braves here.   Never did I view
O'er earth a mightier jarlman,   than is one of you,—
That Hero in his harness: yon Man in weapons dight,
He is no mere retainer,   if tells his face aright,
His peerless port and presence!   But know I must your kin,

Beowulf

Your home, before from hence ye   (as if some spies ye bin)
Farther fare on Daneland.   Ye boatmen of the brine,
Ye far-off dwellers, hear now   this simple thought of mine:
'T were best forthwith ye tell me   whence your comings be!"

IV

Now *as we sit in our banquet hall before our tankards at ease with the thanes (our merry banquet hall, not infested with any Monster as was Heorot), the Scop chants, renewing the notes of his harp, notes he has struck before in other banquet halls.   And he chants the honest reply of Beowulf to the Coast Guard on horseback, and tells how that friendly Coast Guard then guided Beowulf and his fourteen young men-at-arms to King Hrothgar.   And he chants the farewell words of the Coast Guard to Beowulf, when Heorot Hall appeared shining in the distance, and how the Coast Guard wheeled his horse around and returned to his lookout by the sea.*

HIM answered then the eldest,   the war-band Leader, he,
His chest of words unlocking: "Of Geatish kin are we,
And Hyglac's hearth-fellows.   Wide was my father's fame;
The high-born Warrior-Chieftain,   and Ecgtheow his name.
He tarried many winters   before he fared away
From his courts, an old man;   and wide o'er earth today
Him the wise remember.   In faithful mood we come

Beowulf

Seeking the son of Halfdane,　　thy Folk-King at home.
Be to us good of guidance.　　To Danemen's monarch bold,
We have a mickle errand,—　　which must not lurk untold:
Thou wottest if it be so,　　as we have heard for sooth,
That 'mongst ye Danes some dusky　　Scather without ruth,
Some Doer in the dark night,　　is dealing spite uncouth,
Dastard shame and carnage.　　I can in generous mood
Teach a rede to Hrothgar,　　how he, the sage and good,
This Fiend may overmaster,—　　if e'er to be it is
That toil and teen shall alter,　　help come to him and his,
And seething cares grow cooler;　　or else forevermore
He tholeth days of sorrow,　　dearth so sad and sore,
Whilst there upon its high-place　　the best of halls shall bide."
　　The Watchman, doughty servitor,　　from his steed replied:
"Behooveth the keen shieldman,　　he who thinketh well,
'Twixt words and works the tokens　　cunningly to tell.
I hear this band is friendly　　unto the great Scylding:
Bear forth your weeds and weapons;　　I'll guide you to my King,
And bid my faithful kin-thanes　　'gainst aught of foes to guard
Your boat upon the beach here,　　this floater newly-tarred,
Till once more, o'er the sea-streams,　　the curved-neck timber bear
To Weder-mark the dear men,—　　those to whomsoe'er
It shall be granted safely　　to bide the coming fray."
　　They gat them, then, to fare forth;　　at rest the floater lay,
On hawser fast at anchor,　　broad-breasted ship ashore.
O'er cheek-guards shone the golden　　body of the boar—
Flashing, fire-hardened,　　keeping a life-guard o'er
The battle-eager Hero.　　Together on they sped,
Until they saw the gold-bright　　high hall timberéd.
Under the wide heavens,　　where'er men dwell, was that
The fairest of all houses　　wherein King Hrothgar sat;
The light whereof went streaming　　out o'er many lands.

Beowulf

Then showed their Guide that gleaming   burg of battle-bands;
Bade their march be forward,   thither where he show'th;
Reined around his palfrey,   words thereafter quoth:
"Time for me to fare back;   in his mercy may
The Almighty Father   keep ye safe alway
On your voyage and venture.   I will to the coast,
There to hold my sea-watch   'gainst a hostile host."

V

THE *Scop chants how Beowulf and his armed band marched up to the walls
of far-shining Heorot; how Wulfgar, King Hrothgar's Herald, challenged them
in friendly wise; how Beowulf asked him for an audience with the King; and
how Wulfgar, with eager speed, went into the hall and told Hrothgar.*

THE street was laid with bright stones;   the road led on the band;
The battle-byrnies shimmered,   the hard, the linked-by-hand;
The iron-rings, the gleaming,   amid their armor sang,
Whilst thither, in dread war-gear,   to hall they marched alang;
The ocean-weary warriors   set down their bucklers wide,
Their shields, so hard and hardy,   against that House's side;
They stacked points up, these seamen,   their ash-wood, gray-tipped sp
And bent to bench, as clankéd   their byrnies, battle-gears—
An iron-troop well-weaponed!   Then proud a Dane forthwith

Beowulf

Did of these men-at-arms there   enquire the kin and kith:
"Ye bear these plated bucklers   hither from what realms;
These piléd shafts of onset,   gray sarks, and visored helms?
The Henchman and the Herald   of Hrothgar, lo, am I!
Never so many strangers   I've seen of mood more high.
I ween that 't is for prowess,   and not for exile far,
That 't is indeed for glory,   that ye have sought Hrothgár."
   The valor-famed, the proud Prince   of Weders, made reply,
As, hardy under helmet,   he spake his words thereby:
"We're Hyglac's board-fellows,   Beowulf my name.
I would to son of Halfdane   my errand here proclaim,
To the great King, thy Master,   if he but thinketh meet
To grant to us that we may   one so goodly greet."
   Wulfgar made a speech then   (Prince of the Wendels, he,
For soul of war and wisdom   renowned exceedingly):
"Fain will I ask the Danes' Friend,   the Lord of all Scyldings,
As to the boon thou beggest,—   will ask the Breaker-of-Rings,
My ever-glorious Sovran,   touching this thy quest,
And quickly fetch such answer   as he, the good, deems best."
   In haste he hied him thither   where King Hrothgar sate,
The old man, the hoary,   with his jarls in state.
He strode, the valor-faméd,   until he stood before
The shoulders of his dear King—   O he knew courtly lore!
Wulfgar made a speech then   to his chief, Hrothgár:
"Hither have there ferried,   coming from afar
O'er the ocean stretches,   Geatfolk to our hall;
Him who is their eldest   Beowulf they call.
These men-at-arms the boon beg   that they, my Chief, of thee
May ask and hear a word now: O gracious Hrothgar, be
Not niggard of replyings!   They in their warrior-dress
Of jarlman's fairest favor   are worthy, as I guess,—
And he who led them hither   is doughty prince indeed."

Beowulf

VI

THE *Scop strikes his harp again, recounting to us Hrothgar's reply to the Herald,—how Hrothgar had known of Beowulf's lineage, as son of Ecgtheow and grandson of Hrethel, the former King of the Geats (father of the present King, Hygelac), and known too of Beowulf's mighty strength, equal to thirty thanes. Surely Beowulf, said Hrothgar, has come to save us from Grendel. So Wulfgar, the Herald, called from the door that Beowulf and his band should enter. And Beowulf stood before King Hrothgar in Heorot, and announced his errand, with honest pride in his past victories over Monsters and with brave readiness to face this new Monster, Cannibal Grendel. Though Grendel, as he had heard, bore a charmed life against all weapons of mankind, he would trust in his own powerful grip of hand and arm.*

HROTHGAR made his speech then,   Helm of the Scylding-Breed:
"I knew him as a child once;   Ecgtheow his father old,
To whom, at home, Geat Hrethel,   his only daughter gave;
And now is Ecgtheow's offspring,   hither come, the bold,
And seeketh now the faithful   friend across the wave.
Of yore those seamen told me,   who bore to Geatmen's land
Thither in thanks my royal gifts,   that he in grip-of-hand,
He, the keen-at-contest, had   the clinch of thirty thanes.
Him holy God in mercy sent,   methinks, to us West-Danes
Against the greed of Grendel.   This goodly youth unto,

14

Beowulf

I trust to proffer treasure   for this his derring-do.
Be speedy, bid them enter   to see our banded thanes,
Say eke to them in right words   they're welcome guests to Danes."
　　Then went to doorway Wulfgar,   and spake he from within:
"My high Lord, King of East-Danes,   bids say he knows your kin;
And that ye are to him all,   from o'er the ocean crests,
Ye hardy-hearted seamen,   hither welcome guests.
Now may ye under visors   wend in warrior-gear
To see our Hrothgar, leaving   your battle-bucklers here,
Your ash-woods, shafts-of-slaughter,   to bide the parley's close."
　　Uprose the mighty Geat then;   ringed around him, rose
His valiant throng of thanemen.   Some remained without,
Guarding their martial trappings,   as bade their chieftain stout.
They hied them in together,   where the Herald led,
Under roof of Heorot.   The Hero strode ahead,
The stout One under helmet,   till at the hearth he stood.
　　Beowulf made his speech then   (shone his corslet good,
A cunning net-work woven   by olden wit of smith):
"Hail and health, O Hrothgar!   Of Hyglac's kin and kith
Am I, who've gained in young days   glories not a few.
Afar this thing of Grendel   on my home-turf I knew.
Sea-farers say it standeth,   this excelling hall,
Idle and empty   unto each and all,
When under heaven's hollows   the evening-light is hid.
So my best of henchmen,   my canny carls, they did
Teach me, Sovran Hrothgar,   that I should seek thee out,
For that so well they wotted   this strength of mine how stout.
Themselves had they seen me   from sore straits come alive,
Blood-flecked from foemen,   where I'd bounden five,
Killed the kin of ettins,   out upon the main
By night had smote the nicors,   suffered stress and pain,
Avenged their hate of Geatmen—   (they hoped to harry us!)—

Beowulf

And crunched and crushed those grim ones.   And now with Grendel th
With the Grisly, this Giant,   alone I'd hold debate.
So now, O Prince of Bright-Danes,   thou Shelter-of-the-Great,
Of thee one boon I'm begging: O Scyldings' Bulwark-Bar,
Deny not, noble Folk-Friend,   now I have come so far,
That I alone with mine here,   who still would share my lot,
This throng of hardy thanemen,   may purge thee Heorot.
Eke have I learned this Terror,   in wanton mood and vain,
Recketh not of weapons.   Therefore will I disdain
(Thus Hyglac's heart, my Master's,   may it rejoice through me)
To bear or sword or broad shield,   that yellow disk, to strife.
With grip I'll grasp this Grendel,   and we'll contend for life,
A loather 'gainst a loather.   The one whom death shall hale,
Let him believe the Lord's doom.   He will, if he prevail,
Methinketh, in that war-hall,   eat unfearingly
The Geatfolk, as so often   the Danishmen did he.
No need for thee to hide, then,   this head of mine or veil;
He'll have me, sprent with gore, if   't is I whom Death shall hale;
He'll bear his bloody quarry,   he'll think to taste his prey;
He'll eat—this lonely Stalker—   unmournfully away;
He'll track with me his fen-lair: the need will ne'er be thine
In death to have the care of   the body which was mine.
Send Hygelac this war-coat,   which wardeth now my breast
(Of all men's battle-byrnies   the brightest and the best)—
If that Hild should hale me—   Hrethel left in trust,
And smith Weland worked it.   Wyrd goeth as she must."

Beowulf

VII

THE *Scop chants Hrothgar's speech to Beowulf. Hrothgar well remembered Beowulf's father Ecgtheow, for Ecgtheow, having slain a man from another tribe called the Wylfings, had fled even from his own people, the Waegmundings, southward to seek refuge with Hrothgar, long ago when Hrothgar was first King of the Danes. And Hrothgar had settled the trouble by sending gifts to the angry Wylfings and by making Ecgtheow swear oaths to him (with a promise, doubtless, to make no more trouble). Hrothgar saw in Beowulf's coming a son's gratitude for Hrothgar's kindness to his father. Then Hrothgar went on to tell of the fearful wrack and ruin on Heorot wrought long years by Grendel. But hope seemed at hand. The Strong One had come. So Danes and Geats sat together and drank the mead, and the Harper sang clear of voice in Heorot.*

HROTHGAR made his speech then,   Helm of Scylding-Breeds:
"Us hast thou sought, friend Beowulf,   because of ancient deeds,
Because too of thy kindness.   Thy father, when by hand
Heatholaf he slew there   in the Wylfings' land,
The worst of feuds awakened.   Then might his Weder-kin,
For fear of Wylfings' harryings,   take not Ecgtheow in.
Thence he sought the South-Danes,   over the sea-surging,
Us, the Glory-Scyldings,   what time I first was King
Of Danefolk and in youth held   this kingdom jeweléd,
This treasure-burg of heroes.   For Heorogar was dead,
Yes, he, my elder brother,   bairn of Halfdane high,
Was not among the living—   a better man than I!
Thereafter I compounded   the feud for a fee:
I sent unto the Wylfings,   over the ridge of the sea,
Goodly gifts and olden,   and oaths he sware to me.
    Sorrow for soul of me 'tis   to tell to any one
What shame to me, what dread spite,   in Heorot Grendel's done
With his thoughts of hatred;   is my folk-on-floor,

Beowulf

My warrior throng of house-carls,   almost no more.
Them hath Wyrd away swept   into Grendel's greed.
Yet can God that Scather mad   turn from his deed!
Full oft across their ale-cups   my men-at-arms would pledge,
When beer had roused their bosoms,   to bide with fierce sword-edge,
Within these walls of wassail,   Grendel's coming-on.
But then would be this mead-house,   when the day would dawn,
This lordly chamber, gore-stained   at the morning-tide;
Boards of all its benches   with blood be-spattered wide,
With battle-blood this hall here.   I had of trusty men,
Of dear and doughty, fewer—   since death had taken them.
Sit thee now to banquet,   the cords of speech untie,
Tell us of thy victor-vaunt,   as whets thy soul thereby."
    Then for Geatish tribesmen,   close together all,
Was a bench made ready   in the wassail-hall.
There the stout-in-spirit   went to take their seat,
Proud of this their prowess.   A henchman did as meet,
Mindful he to bear round   the figured ale-tankárd,
And pour to each the clear mead.   Whiles would sing a bard,
Clear of voice in Heorot.   Revelled there the thanes—
A host of happy heroes,   Wederfolk and Danes.

Beowulf

VIII

THE *Scop now chants an interlude of quarrelsome words.   It seems that Un-ferth (whose name meant 'Un-peace'), Hrothgar's Adviser and Spokesman, was at once jealous of the bold Stranger.   Yes, Unferth had heard of this Beowulf —how Beowulf had been woefully beaten by Breca in a famous swimming match of seven nights and days out on the wild ocean along the Coast of the land we now call Scandinavia.   So it's not likely, said Unferth, that Beowulf will be of much account against Grendel.   But the Scop gives us anon Beowulf's straight-forward reply, which told the great truth of that marvelous adventure, the gen-erous rivalry and the mutual aid, and the terrors of Water Monsters.*

UNFERTH made his speech then,   at Hrothgar's feet who sate;
   Let loose that bairn of Ecglaf   his secret grudge of hate.
Beowulf's quest, bold seaman,   to him was mickle spite,
Because he might not own it   that any other wight
Ever in this Middle-Yard   more deeds of bravery
Had done beneath the heavens   than himself had he:
"Art thou, then, that Beowulf,   who strove with Breca, thou,
Who on the deep contested   in swimming hard enow!—
When in your pride ye twain did   attempt the waters wide,
And risked in rash vain-glory   your lives upon the tide?
Nor might not any man then,   whether lief or loath,
From fearful voyage dissuade ye,   from breasting seaward both;
There ye stretched your arms out   ocean streams among,
Measured ye the mere's path,   drew with your hands along,
Bounded over the billows.   Flood was asurge with foam,
With the waves of winter.   Ye on the water's home,
Seven nights ye swinkéd.   He outstripped in stroke!
Had the more of might, he!   Him, when morrow broke,
Surf up-cast by Heathoreams.   He sought his home therewith,
He, beloved of clansmen;   sought dear Bronding-kith,

Beowulf

And his own fair stronghold,   where he had a folk,
Had a town and treasures.   All his vaunt 'gainst thee
Did the son of Beanstan   fulfil faithfully!
So I ween for thee now   worser outcome there
(Though in battle-onset,   though in grim warfare,
E'er wert thou so doughty!),   if thou durst abide,
For coming-close of Grendel,   one night-long tide."
   Beowulf made his speech then,   the son of Ecgtheow, he:
"Aplenty hast thou prated,   beer-drunken as thou be,
Friend Unferth, about Breca,—   his feat hast told at length.
But truth I hold it, mine was   a mightier ocean-strength,
A bigger toil in the billows,   than any other man's.
We twain, when still but younglings,   had talked and pledged our plans
To risk (we were but boys then)   our lives far out to sea.
We did as we had vowed to!   Our naked swords had we,
Our hardy swords, in hands there,   on breasting seaward both,
To fend us from the whale-fish.   He could no whit from me
Float o'er the sea-flood swifter—   and I from him was loath.
Thus were we twain together   five nights upon the wave,
Till surge and weltering waters   us both asunder drave;
The coldest of all weathers,   dark night and northern blast,
Blew battle-grim against us;   fierce were the floods we passed;
Roused was the wrath of mere-fish;   but there against the foe
My mail-coat, hard and hand-linked,   helped me even so!
My braided sark-of-battle   lay about my breast,
My corslet gold-adornéd.   Me bottom-ward did wrest
A spotted Devil-Scather—   fast held the Grim his grip!
But unto me was given   to pierce with swordsmanship,
Aye, with the blade-of-battle,   the Monster of the brine.
The mighty Mere-Beast foundered   through this hand of mine!

Beowulf

IX

The Scop continues to chant Beowulf's story of the outcome of the swimming match with Breca. That was the greatest swimming ever done by man (but not the only time that Beowulf was mighty in swimming, as we shall hear later). 'Such prowess,' said Beowulf to Unferth, 'had never been shown by thee; and, if thou wert as good as thy boasts, Grendel would never have wrought such slaughter in Heorot.' And just as Unferth had heard of Beowulf before, so Beowulf had heard of Unferth, since rumor and story were borne in those days by sailors and gleemen's ballads back and forth from tribe to tribe. Yes, Beowulf could silence Unferth by reminding him that he was known to have slain his own brothers. 'Enough of him; let the Danes trust in me, Beowulf, the Geat.' And thus the feasting went on, and Wealhtheow, the Queen (for the high-born ladies joined in those days the feasting of the warriors), gave the ale-cup to the King, and to each and all, and to Beowulf himself. And Beowulf addressed Wealh-theow, Hrothgar's Queen, avowing his purpose once more. And, then, after the feasting, as night was drawing on, the clan arose and Hrothgar gave over the Watch in Heorot to Beowulf and his men. Will Unferth forgive Beowulf, or will he wait his chances to do Beowulf a harm and thus keep the Strong One from freeing Heorot forever of Cannibal Grendel? The Scop will tell you all.

THUS the loathly lurkers   pressed me sore and oft.
I served them with my dear sword   in ways not soft.
For those foul devisers   the hope of fill was o'er—
To eat me, to sit round   a feast on ocean's floor!

21

Beowulf

But upon the morrow, wounded by the glaive,
They were lying up along the leavings of the wave,
Put to sleep by sword there— ne'er to thwart again
Sailor-folk in ferrying the fords of the main.
From the east a light rose— God's beacon bright;
The rolling seas subsided, so that see I might
Headlands and windy walls. Wyrd will often save
A jarl who is no fey man, if he be but brave.
And so to me 't was granted that with sword I slew
Nine there of the Nicors. Nay, I never knew
Under the vault of the heavens by night a fight more fierce,
Nor on the streams of the ocean a man put to it worse.
Way-weary, yet I 'scapéd the clutch of monsters fell;
And the sea up-cast me, flood-tide and swell,
On the land of Finn-men. Never about thee
Such straits of strife, such terrors of sword-blades heard I tell;
Ne'er yet at war-play Breca, nor neither one of ye,
Did deed so bold with bloody brands— nor boast thereof I will—
Though thou forsooth thy brothers, thy kin-of-heart, didst kill!
(Whence curse of hell awaits thee, though good thy wit may be.)
I say to thee in sooth now, thou of Ecglaf son,
That Grendel ne'er so many gruesome things had done,
The Grisly ne'er such havoc in Heorot to thy King,
If thought of thine, if soul of thine, were grim as thy telling.
But he hath found he needeth fear or feud or stroke
Little from thy people, the Victor-Scylding folk!
He taketh the forced pledges, unsparingly he rends,
He hath his lust of slaughter, he puts to sleep, he sends,—
He recketh not of any contest with the Dane.
But speedily 't is mine now to show him might and main,
The warrior-work of Geatmen! Let him go who can
Blithe to mead tomorrow— when o'er bairns of man

22

Beowulf

Shineth from the southward,   on other day begun,
Once more that light-of-morning,   the sky-girt sun."
   Then the Prince of Bright-Danes,   the Treasure-Breaker, he,
The old-haired and war-famed,   had his time of glee.
Now in help he trusted;   from Beowulf he caught,
He, his people's Shepherd,   the firm-resolvéd thought.
Then was there heroes' laughter;   and rang the shout and song,
And merry speech was bandied;   and then stepped forth along
Wealhtheow, Queen of Hrothgar,   mindful of manners all,
And gold-bedight she greeted   the guest-men in the hall.
And then the high-born Lady   erst gave the cup in hand
To him who was the Warder   of East-Danes' fatherland;
And him she bade be blithesome   at the bout-of-beer,
Him beloved of clansmen.   He took with goodly cheer
The banquet and the beaker,   the King of victory-fame.
Then round the hall to each and all   she stepped, the Helmings' Dame,
And gave to young and older   the goblet rich-beseen,
Till came the happy moment   when in hall the Queen,
Crown-bedight and high-souled,   the cup to Beowulf bore.
She greeted the Geats' lord;   God she thanked therefor,
Wise in her word-craft,   that her wish had thriven
That she could trust some jarlman   for help 'gainst horrors given.
He took the cup from Wealhtheow,   a warsman fierce-to-smite;
And then he offered answer,   eager for the fight.
   Beowulf made his speech then,   bairn of Ecgtheow, he:
"When with my troop of tribesmen,   I mounted on the sea,
And sate me in my sailor-boat,   I had this thought in me:
Either to work for all time   thy people's will at last,
Or to fall afighting   in grip of Grendel fast.
Firm am I to do my   jarlman's deed withal,
Or to dree my end-of-days   in this mead-hall."
   Those words well pleased that woman,—   the Geatman's battle-vows;

Beowulf

And gold-bedight she went, then,   to sit beside her spouse,
Folk-Queen high-born.   And once again there be
Brave words spoken,   and hall-men in glee,
And uproar of victor-folk—   until the King anon
Would seek his evening resting-place,   Halfdane's Son.
He knew that battle waited   the fiend on that high floor,
After they the sun-light   could see no more,
After the dun night   was over all about,
And the shapes of shadow   should come aprowling out,
Wan beneath the welkin.   Together rose the clan;
Then Hrothgar greeted Beowulf,   man wishing luck to man,
Gave him of that wine-house   the power and sway, and swore:
"Never have I trusted   to any man before,—
Not since I could heave up   hand and shield of me,—
This brave house of Danemen,   until now to thee.
Have now and hold it—   this excelling hall!
Remember thy glory,—   make known thy might to all!
Watch against the Wrathful!   Each wish of thine I'll do,
If with thy life thou see'st   this deed of daring through."

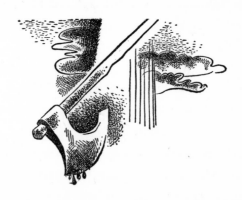

Beowulf

X

THE *Scop chants how Beowulf undid his armor in Heorot, and made his boast ere he laid himself down upon the mead-bench that stretched along the side wall. He again vaunted he would use no weapon except his own main strength, for in those days to speak out frankly one's own good opinion of one's self was not counted an unseemly thing. Then, while the other young Geatmen slumbered, Beowulf lay on his pillow, apparently slumbering too, but really very much awake. And Grendel was making toward Heorot.*

THEN did Hrothgar hie him,　the Scyldings' Bulwark-Bar,
Forth from the mead-hall　with his band-of-war;
Wished that Warrior-Chieftain　Wealhtheow for to seek,
His Queen for his bed-mate.　The King-of-Glory there
Over against Grendel　(so men had heard him speak)
Had set a chamber-warder;　whose special task was care
Of him, the Danemen's Monarch,　in keeping ogre-guard.
Truly, the Geatish Leader　trusted well the Lord,
And his own proud mettle.　His mail he then undid,
From his head his helmet,　gave his figured sword
(That goodliest of iron-things)　to his man and bid
Watch and ward his war-gear.
　　　　　　　　　　Then his boast he said,
Beowulf, the brave Geat,　ere he clomb to bed:
"Not poorer in battle-prowess,　do I reckon me,
In the works of warfare,　than is Grendel, he!
So not with sword I purpose　to spill his life tonight,
To put to sleep the Monster,　though indeed I might.
Those goodly arts he knows not　whereby to cut at me,
To hew against my buckler,　though so bold he be
In the works of combat.　But this eventide
To both of us behooveth　leave the blade aside,

Beowulf

If he durst to seek out   a lack-weapon fray,
And holy Lord, the wise God,   thereafter either way
Let him decree the glory   as him-thinketh best."
   And then the Keen-in-contest   laid him down to rest;
And in the pillow sank, then,   that Jarlman's cheek and head;
And many a brisk one round him   bent to his hall-bed—
Many an ocean-warrior.   Not any of the band
Thought 't would e'er be his to seek   from here his fatherland,
The dear folk, or free-burg,   that fostered him and bore;
But they had heard that ere now   more than many a man
Slaughter-death had taken off   of the Danish clan.
But unto them the Lord gave   the webs of weal-in-war,
Gave unto the Weders   aid and comfort so
That, through the strength of One, they   all o'ercame their foe,—
Through his might of selfhood.   'T is known that God, the Giver,
Hath wielded over mankind   forever and forever.
   Striding through the wan night,   the Shadow-Stalker stepped;
The holders of that hornéd house,   the shooting-men, they slept—
All, save only one there.   'T was known to men that he,
That ghostly Scather, might not,   against the Lord's decree,
Draw them down to Darkness.   Watching the foe to smite,
In wrath the Geatman bided   the issue of the fight.

Beowulf

XI

THE *Scop strikes louder notes upon his harp and he chants with so much fire that we in our banquet hall keep our hands fixed in the handles of our tankards and forget to drink.   For he tells how Grendel burst the door of Heorot, greedy for man-flesh and unwitting the welcome he would get, and how Grendel ate up a sleeping Geat, and how, to his eternal sorrow, he then laid paws upon Beowulf. Fierce indeed was that wrestling, and it was a wonder that Heorot, so battered and shaken, did not tumble down on the heads of all.   And the Danes, who were waiting yonder on the wall of the Burg, heard the night-shrieks of Grendel in the grip of the Strong One.*

AND now from out the moorland,   under the misty slopes,
    Came astalking Grendel—   God's anger on his hopes.
That Scather foul was minded   to snare of human kin
Some one, or sundry,   that high hall within.
Under the welkin strode he,   until full well he spied
The wine-house, the gold-hall,   with fret-work glittering wide.
Nor was that the first time   Hrothgar's home he sought.
Yet never in his life-days,   late or early, aught
Like this harsh welcome found he   from thanemen in the hall.
He came afooting onward   to the house withal,
This warring One that ever   had been from bliss out-cast;
Forthwith the door sprang open,   with forgéd-bolts though fast,
When with his paws he pressed it;   yea, then, on bale-work bent,
Swoln as he was with fury,   that house's mouth he rent.
Anon the Fiend was treading   the shining floor in there;
On he moved in anger;   from eyes of him did glare,
Unto fire likest,   a light unfair.
He saw within the chamber   many a man asleep,—
Kinsman band together,   of clanfolk a heap;
Laughed his mood, was minded   that Hobgoblin grim,

Beowulf

Ere the dawn to sunder   each his life from limb,
Now that fill-of-feeding   he weened awaited him!
But Wyrd it was that would not   longer grant him might
To seize on more of mankind   after that same night.

    Was watching he, the stalwart   Kin of Hygelac,
How with grip the Grisly   would go at his attack.
He had no thought, this Goblin,   that business to put off;
But pounced upon a sleeping man,   starting quick enough!
Unthwartedly he slit him,   bit his bone-box, drunk
From his veins the blood of him,   gulped him chunk by chunk,
Till soon, then, he had there   this un-living Geat
Altogether eaten down,   even to hands and feet.
Then stepped he forth and nearer,   and pawed by bed to nim
The hardy-headed Hero,   reaching toward him
With his claws be-deviled: with thoughts that boded harm,
Beowulf received him,   propped upon an arm.
But soon he found, did Grendel,—   this Herdsman-over-crimes,—
That never in this Middle-World,   this earth of many climes,
He'd met a mightier hand-grip   in any man than here.
Afeared in mood and spirit,   small help he gat from fear!
Was bent on making-off, ho!—   out to the dark would flee,
Would seek the din of devils!   Not now in Heorot he
Fared as in the old-days!—   And then the Bold-in-pride,
Hyglac's Thane, remembered   his speech of eventide.
Up he stood and grasped him   so tight the fingers cracked.
The Ettin started outward—   the Jarl upon him packed.
The monstrous One was minded,   whereso'er he may,
To fling himself but farther,   and from thence away
To flee to boggy dingles;   his fingers' power he wist
Was in the grip of Grim One.   That was a sorry quest
Whereon the Scather Grendel   to Heorot Hall had pressed.
The lordly room resounded;   and all the Danes did quail,

Beowulf

Those warrior jarls of walled-town,   lest reft for aye of ale.
Wroth were the ramping twain there,   those warders of the house;
The chamber rang with uproar;   mickle wonder 't was
How the wine-hall held out   'gainst shock of fighters there,
How adown did fall not   that earthly dwelling fair.
But inside and outside   it was too firmly wrought,
With the bands of iron,   forged by cunning thought.
I've heard that many a mead-bench,   with gold gilded o'er,
There where tugged the foemen,   started from the floor.
So had weened the wise ones   of the Scyldings erst
That never any man by force   might asunder burst
That brave house and bone-bright,   nor by craft might split—
Save that bosoming fire   in flame should swallow it.

    Up there rose a shriek then,   strange enough o'night;
On each and every North-Dane   seized a grisly fright,
On each who from the wall there   heard that 'well-a-way'—
Heard this God-Forsaker   chant his gruesome lay,
His song of loss-in-battle,   heard bewail his wound
This Grendel, Hell's Bondsman.   For held him tightly bound
That man who was of all men   between the seas confessed,
In the days of this our life here,   in strength the mightiest.

Beowulf

XII

THE *Scop chants how Beowulf's men hacked in vain at Grendel with their an-cestral swords, apparently forgetting in their fury and terror what Beowulf had said, that Grendel bore a charmed life against all weapons of mankind. But Beo-wulf at last tore out Grendel's arm, and the wounded Monster fled forth into the night to die in his dark, murky fens; and Beowulf hung the bloody trophy under the roof of Heorot—as it would seem, on the outside just over the door.*

THE jarls' Defender would not,   forsooth with a will,
Let him loose aliving—   him who came to kill,
Deeming not his life-days   of use to any folk.
More than once did jarlman   of Beowulf try a stroke
With his father's falchion,   fain the life to ward
Of the faméd Chieftain,   their great Lord.
They wist not, these warsmen,   these hardy-headed few,
The while they fell asmiting   and thought the while to hew
On this side, on that side,   seeking soul to kill,
That best of earthly iron blades,   nor never battle-bill,
This accurséd Scather   could hurt or harm:
For over victor-weapons   he had cast a charm,
Over every sword-edge.   Yet his passing-o'er,
In the days of his life here,   was to be full sore;
And this alien Elf-Thing   was to fare afar
To the under-places   where the devils are.
For he had found, had Grendel,—   this Striver against God,—
Who in such merry mood of old   so oft on man had trod,
That his bulk-of-body   would not help him moe,
Now Hygelac's stout Kinsman   held his fore-paw so!
Was each unto the other   alive a loathly thing.
A body-sore he gat there,   this wretched Ogreling:
There showed upon his shoulder   a cureless wound anon;

Beowulf

His sinews sprang asunder;   from socket burst the bone.
To Beowulf was given   the glory of the fray;
And Grendel was to flee hence,   sick-to-death, away,—
Off under fen-slopes,   off to dens of gloom.
He wist, O well he wist it,   his end-of-life had come,
His full tale of days now.—   The wish of Danemen all,
After that gory set-to,   had come to pass withal.

    He had now y-cleanséd,   he who came from far,
The Wise-Head and Stout-Heart,   the House of high Hrothgár,
Had freed it now from fury.   His night-work made him glad,
His deed of might and glory.   The Geatmen's Leader had
Now before the East-Danes   fulfilled his vaunting there,—
Aye, all ills amended   and the carking care,
Which they had dreed aforetime,   and by stress and strain
Long been doomed to suffer—   more than little pain.
Of this there was a token,   clear enough in proof,
When the Victor-Fighter   under the gabled roof
Hung on high the fore-paw,   the arm and shoulder grim—
And there ye had together   all Grendel's clutching-limb!

Beowulf

XIII

THE Scop chants how chiefs and thanes from round about rode to Heorot, an
how they then followed on their horses the bloody trail of Grendel to the mere o
the Nicors, the Water Monsters, and how they galloped back for another look a
Grendel's paw, sometimes racing for sheer joy and sometimes listening to th
ballads sung by one of their number along the road. Our Scop tells us that on
song was made up then and there, in praise of Beowulf's quest; and this se
us to wondering whether Beowulf was with the party or whether, wearied by h
watch and his work in the night, he had remained at the Burg or at Heorot t
sleep a sound sleep. Our Scop then gives us the substance of another ballad sun
by the Scop in the story. This was about another hero, Sigemund, who had slai
a Dragon and rifled its gold-hoard (even as Beowulf was himself to slay a Drago
sometime and rifle its hoard). And this ballad reminds our Scop of an old Danis
King, Heremod (before the coming of Scyld and Hrothgar's line), who is men
tioned several times in the poem for his cruelty and feuds, especially in contras
to such fine, generous aethelings as Sigemund and Beowulf. But if we don'
understand the allusions to such folk-characters as Sigemund and Heremo
never mind; for some wiser heads today don't altogether understand them eithe
though those who used to listen in the old days surely understood them and like
them. For bygone men knew many legends well that even the wisest men o
today, by the hardest study of old books in Anglo-Saxon, in Old Icelandic, or i
Mediaeval Latin, can often only partly puzzle out. Perhaps we will do better t
ask the Scop to omit such digressions and to tell us only about Beowulf himsel
Or if he won't omit them, we have a right not to pay any attention till he come
back to the main story.

THEN there was at morning   —so I 've heard the tale—
    Round about the gift-hall   many a man-of-mail.
Thither fared the folk-chiefs,   near and far asunder,
All along the wide-ways,   for to view the wonder,—
The traces of the loathed Thing.   Seemed his passing-out

Beowulf

Not a grievous sorrow   to any thereabout,
Any who were viewing   now the craven's trail—
How he, weary-hearted,   beaten in the bout,
Death-doomed and routed,   off away from here
Made for very life his tracks   to the Nicors' mere.
Yonder were the waters   weltering with blood;
Mingled all with hot gore,   surged the gruesome flood;
With battle-spatter rolled the deep,   where the death-doomed then
Laid forlorn his body down,   his heathen soul, in fen—
There did Hell receive him!
                         Home on horse anew
Rode the old companions,   many a younger too,
Back from merry journey,   bold men back from mere,
Warriors on the white steeds.   Then was sounded clear
Beowulf's deed of daring: all said it o'er and o'er,
That south or north none other,   from shore to farthest shore,
Betwixt the seas none other,   beneath the sky's domain,
Was better man to bear shield   or worthier to reign.
(Nor they by this belied not   their Friend in anything,
Hrothgar, their gracious Lord—   but that was goodly King!)
   Whiles these doughty warsmen   let leap their fallow bays,
Let run a race where fairest   seemed the country-ways;
Whiles a thane of Hrothgar,—   a man of boasts was he,
Stored with olden sagas,   and deft at balladry,—
Found one good word for other   and bound them soothfully;
So too this scop made mention   right well of Beowulf's quest,
And had good speed at speaking   his phrases artfullest,
Linking words together.
                         [He told an unknown story—
All he'd heard of Sigemund,   of his deeds of glory:
The warring of the Waelsing,   his wanderings so wide,
The feuds and the betrayals,   whereof no men beside

33

Beowulf

Wist aught but only Fitela—   when he to him would tell,
The uncle to the nephew,   somewhat of what befell;
For ever stood they comrades   in need against the foe,
And countless of the ettin-kin   they had with sword laid low.
After his death, for Sigemund   upsprang a fame not least
When he, that hardy warsman,   had quelled that Serpent-Beast,
That Guardian of the gold-hoard.   Under the hoary stone
Dared he, the son of aetheling,   that bold deed alone—
For Fitela was with him not.   Yet luck to him was given,
That this wondrous dragon   so by sword was riven
That the lordly steel with point   the cavern wall did pierce.
The drake he died a slaughter-death.   And Sigemund, the fierce,
Had gained by prowess power   to use at will the hoard;
A sea-boat he loaded;   the rings he bare aboard;
He bare to the ship's bosom,   this man whom Waels begot,
That gold-gleaming treasure.—   But Dragon melted hot!
Chief was he of outlaws,   through tribes anear and far,
For the deeds of daring,   this warriors' Bulwark-Bar
(And so erewhile he prospered)—   yes, chief since waned away
The battle-strength of Heremod,   his force and fame in fray.
For Heremod was lured forth,   when mid the Jutes was he,
Into the power of foemen,   and sent off speedily.
Too long the waves of sorrow   had lamed this man of strife;
To jarls, to all the aethelings,   he'd been a care for life.
And often in the old days,   the wanderings of their chief
Had been to his sage vassals   a weary thing of grief,—
To many a one who'd trusted   he'd be a help from harm,
Prosper as a king's bairn,   achieve his father's arm,
And folk and hoard and stronghold   guard from hostile band—
This kingdom of the heroes,   the Scyldings' fatherland.
Therein the Kin of Hygelac   a fairer virtue showed
To all, to friends, to all mankind—   than crime-curst Heremod.]

Beowulf

So homeward, oft aracing,   these warriors old and young
With swift horses followed   the fallow paths along.
Now was the sun-of-morning urged   higher up the skies;
Went many a bold retainer   to see the wondrous prize
At the high hall Heorot.   The King himself no less,
The Warder of the ring-hoard,   famed for worthiness,
From out the wedding-bowers   strode in royal sheen,
Girt by many clansmen;   and, lo, with him the Queen
With troop of maidens measured   the mead-path to the scene.

XIV

THE *Scop chants on, for he knows his harp and his story well, without sheet of music or page of books; and he chants now the speech of Hrothgar to Beowulf, before the Hall of Heorot where hung Grendel's arm and paw for Queen Wealhtheow and Spokesman Unferth and all to see. And Hrothgar adopted Beowulf as his own son. Then the Scop chants Beowulf's answer to Hrothgar. It was a manly answer; yet we are disappointed that Beowulf did not thank Hrothgar for praising and adopting him. Perhaps Beowulf was so full of the fight that could think of nothing else.*

HROTHGAR made a speech then;   he walked unto the hall;
   Stood upon the fore-steps;   looked at roof so tall,
So garnishéd with gold-work;   at Grendel's paw looked he:
"Thanks to the All-Wielder   at once for what I see!

Beowulf

From Grendel have I suffered   such gruesome plight and plunder:
But ever God he worketh   wonder upon wonder—
He is the King-of-Glory!   It was but now that I
Weened no boot for sorrows   for me until I die,
When stood this best of houses   battle-sprent with gore,
A sorrow spread so widely   for every councillor
Who weened they might not ever   save from Fiends-of-murk,
From ogres and from demons,   this great folk-work.
Now hath a thane by Lord's might   a deed put through
That we for all our cunning   erewhile could never do.
Well can she say, that woman   (if yet she be on earth)
Who gave, among the tribes of men,   to such an offspring birth,
That olden God was kindly   to her in child-bearing.
Now Beowulf, best of battlers,   to my heart's fostering
For mine own son I'll take thee.   Guard it well from now,
This our new-born kinship!   Never lack shalt thou
For aught of world's desires   whereover I have power.
Full oft did I for less deed   of old a largesse shower,
Rewards from out my treasure,   upon a punier swain,
A slacker one at slaughter.   By thine own might and main
Thou hast thyself achievéd   that thy name shall live
Forever unto ages.   May the All-Wielder give
Reward of good unto thee,   as ever he hath done."
    Beowulf made a speech then,   who was of Ecgtheow son:
"We wrought that work of warfare,   that fight, with goodly will;
Boldly we dared the might of   that mystic Thing-of-ill.
O I would the rather   that thou his very self
Hadst seen in his trappings,   that weary, wavering Elf!
Swift I thought to pin him   with my clutches firm
Down upon a bed of death,   that he in vain should squirm,
Dying under hand-grip—   unless his body fled.
That flight I could not hinder—   God willed him free instead.

Beowulf

To him, this Life-Destroyer,   I clave not well enough—
He was too strong at foot-work,   this Fiend in making-off!
To save his life, however,   he left his fingers back,
His arm and his shoulder,   as witness of his track!
Yet by this the creature   not any comfort wins;
None the longer lives he,   harried by his sins.
But him his sore hath bounden   fast by bonds of bale,
In a gripe of anguish.   There abide he shall,
Outlawed by evil,   the day of doom so grim,
Waiting how the shining Judge   wills to sentence him!"
　Then Unferth, son of Ecglaf,   he was less noisy wight,
In brag of works of battle,   when, thanks to this man's might,
The aethelings were gazing   that high roof along
At paw and foeman's fingers—   and foreward there they hung,
Each of the claws in place there,   unto steel most like—
That heathen creature's hand-spur,   that warrior's eery spike.
The gazers vowed no brave man's   good old blade soever
Might touch him, might the Monster's   bloody fight-paw sever.

Beowulf

XV

THE *Scop chants how men with busy women-folk set Heorot Hall to right
and gloriously decked it for another feast. Feasting and song and battle and sleep
—the ale-cup, the harp, the good sword, the pillow,—seem to have taken up all
the time of these high-born Danishmen. But no, not all the time; for there was
always time too for the giving of presents and for the making of speeches. Here
the Scop tells us of Hrothgar's rich gifts to Beowulf, the gleaming war-gear and
the caparisoned horses, which were brought before the Hero right then and there
in Heorot Hall. All were merry, and Hrothulf, Hrothgar's nephew, was still
friendly, though the people who used to listen to the story knew that later he
slew Hrethric, Hrothgar's son; and, knowing this, they could feel a sense of
doom, like a shadow, over the bright scene. Our Scop likes to touch the joys of
men with shadows,—likes to remind us of the ironies of fate that dog, unseen,
the footsteps of our mirth.*

THEN quick the hest was given.   Within was Heorot then
  By many hands bedeckéd.   Of women and of men
Aye, full many were there   who did make ready all
That wine-house and guest-room.   Gleamed on every wall
Woven hangings, gold-gay—   of wondrous sights so much,
For each and every mortal   of those who gaze at such.
It had been greatly battered,   that building brave and bright,
Though all within-ward bounden   by bands of iron tight;
And the door-hinges rended;   the roof alone held out
Sound all-together,   when Grendel turned about,
That Ogre in his fleeing,   outlawed by deeds of ill,
And of his life in wanhope.   Ah, let each try who will,
It is not over-easy   to flee away from death!
But each of bairns of mankind,   each who beareth breath,
Each who dwelleth on the ground,   shall seek, as fate shall force,
The place made ready for him,   where his body-corse

Beowulf

Shall sleep upon its resting-bed,   when the feasting's done.
   'T was time and tide when hall-ward hied   Halfdane's son;
The King himself, this Hrothgar,   would in the revel share.
Ne'er heard I tell of tribesmen   themselves who better bare
Around their treasure-giver,   in a goodlier press.
They bent them to the benches,   owners of success!
Merrily they feasted;   took again, again,
Cheerily the mead-cup.   And kinsmen still withal
Were both of those stout-hearted ones   in that high hall—
Hrothgar and Hrothulf.   Within was Heorot then
Filled alone with friends all—   never in those times
Had the folk of Scyldings   wrought the traitor-crimes.
   Then the bairn of Halfdane,   to Beowulf he gave
A banneret of gold-work,   broidered on a stave,
A helmet and a byrnie,   as meed of victory.
And a glorious jewelled sword   many there did see
Borne unto the Hero.   Standing forth on floor,
Beowulf received the cup;   that warrior-band before,
He needed not to suffer shame   for these gifts of price.
I have not known many   to give in friendlier wise
To others on the ale-bench   golden treasures four!
Across the crown of the helmet,   a ridge outside there rose,
Of wires interwoven,   to guard the head from blows,
Lest the files'-remainders,   the battle-hardened glaive,
Too fiercely might scathe it,   what time the brave
Behind his shield should hie him   forth against his foes.
Bade then the jarlmen's Bulwark   bring adown the hall
Horses eight, with golden plate   upon the cheeks of all.
On one a saddle rested   with jewel-work replete,
Shining with deft devices—   that was the battle-seat
Of Hrothgar, the high King,   when Halfdane's son would fare
Forth unto the sword-play;   and in the vanward ne'er

Beowulf

Failed his famous valor,   while round him fell the slain!
And then the Lord of Ingwines   to Beowulf gave the twain,
The horses and the weapons,   as his to have and hold—
Bade him well enjoy them!   Hrothgar, the bold,
The Hoard-Guard of heroes,   so manfully paid back,
With horses and with treasures,   Beowulf's attack,
That none who'll speak the truth aright   can blame for any lack.

XVI

THE *Scop chants how Hrothgar gave gifts also to all Beowulf's fourteen companions, and then makes some pious remarks, as he often does in the course of his story. He then tells us that the Harper in the Hall sang a lay—which may be called "The Woe of Hildeburh." He doesn't give, as in the case of the story of Sigemund, merely the gist of it; but he seems to be repeating the Harper's song word for word. It is quite a story by itself; and not very clear to us today—all about a feud between Danes and Frisians and Jutes, broken faith, battle in a Hall, vengeance, funeral pyres, and a sad-hearted Queen. Many wise men of today have striven to puzzle it out—and each thinks he has succeeded, but they don't all agree with one another and they despise one another grievously for their differences of opinion. Now, in the best interests of good-breeding and toleration for one another, I suggest that we don't listen to "The Woe of Hildeburh" at all —lest we too fall to quarreling over its meaning. But do listen to the spirited ballad some other Scop made on a part of the story, the fight at the doors of the Hall.*

Beowulf

THEN, too, the Lord of jarlmen   at mead-bench bestowed
On each who had with Beowulf   taken the ocean-road
Some treasure, some heirloom,   and bade with gold requite
The death of him whom Grendel   had foully slain that night—
As more of them he fain had slain,   except that God, the good,
And the man's own courage,   for them that wyrd withstood.
The Judge then ruled all races   even as he doth yet—
So best is always insight,   and forethought of wit.
How much of lief and loathly   shall fall to each man's life
Who long makes earth his dwelling here   in these days of strife!
    Now was there chant and music,   together linked as one,
Before the Army-Chieftain,   Halfdane's Son.
The merry harp was fingered,   the lay was lilted free,
As Hrothgar's bard by mead-bench   sang in hall his glee.

THE WOE OF HILDEBURH

["The Hero of the Halfdanes,   Hnaef of Scylding-folk,
In the Frisian struggle   fell by fatal stroke
At the hands of sons of Finn   when they in terror woke.
Little cause had Hildeburh   to praise the Jutemen's troth:
Blameless bereaved was she   of her dear ones both—
Her bairn and her brother,   at the linden-play.
Wounded by the lances,   to doom dropped they.
That was a grieving Princess,   and she, the daughter of Hoc,
Had good cause to mourn her fate   when the morning broke,
And under the skies she set her eyes   on murder-bale of kin,—
There, O where in all the world   her greatest joys had been.
    The fray took off the thanes of Finn,   all but only few;
He might not in the parley-place   'gainst Hengest battle do,
Nor save by fight from Prince's Wight   the remnants of his crew.
And so did they, the Frisians,   a truce with Danemen call:

Beowulf

They'd yield another floor to them,   a high-seat and hall,
And Danes with bairns of Jutemen   should each rule half of all;
And Finn, the son of Folcwald,   should, with gifts of pay,
Do the Danemen honor   each and every day;
Should, with his ring-giving,   favor Hengest's men,—
With costly boon of fretted gold,   as much as Hengest then
In beer-hall should cheer all   the folk of Frisian kin.
Then did they swear a peace-pact,   unalterable for both;
Finn did unto Hengest vow,   without all strife, on oath:
That, with his Witan's counsel,   he'd use Hnaef's remnant right;
That no man there, by word or work,   should break the pact they p
Nor Frisians e'er should speak thereof,   by any evil sleight,
Though Danes, bereft of ruler,   in their need now were
Followers of the man that slew   Hnaef, their Ring-Givér;
And if then any Frisian   should by foemen's taunt
Of old hate and slaughter   to the Danemen vaunt,
Straight should it be settled then   by the edge of sword.
  The oath was sworn, the costly gold   uplifted from the hoard,
The best of braves of War-Danes,   Hnaef, on the pile lay stark;
Upon that pyre was plain to sight   the gore-bespattered sark,
His swine all golden,—   the boar-crest iron-strong,—
And aethelings, by wounds dead,—   for they had fallen, a throng.
And Hildeburh behested   that at Hnaef's own pyre
The bairn of her own body   be given unto the fire,
His bone and brawn be burned there   and laid upon the pile,
By the uncle's shoulder.   The lady wept the while;
Bemoaning in dirges.   Her warrior-son they raise.
There wound unto the welkin   a huge bale's blaze,
And crackled at the grave-mound.   Heads did melt asunder;
Gashes burst and blood sprang   from death-wounds under.
Flame, of spirits greediest,   did all of those devour,
Of either folk, whom war had ta'en.   Gone was their flower.]

Beowulf

XVII

OUR *Scop brings the Harper's story of "The Woe of Hildeburh" to an end.
And he goes on to tell how Wealhtheow, Hrothgar's Queen, addressed her Con-
sort, making a hopeful allusion to Hrothulf in Hrothulf's very presence. She
could not know that in the future Hrothulf was going to slay her son Hrethric,
though she may have felt some anxiety that sometime all might not be well. And
Beowulf was seated between Hrethric and his brother Hrothmund, being now
himself their brother by adoption. And Unferth, the quarrelsome and jealous,
was happy too, seated, as was his wont, at the feet of the King; but perhaps it
was none other than he who later stirred up the trouble between Hrothgar and
Hrothulf that resulted in the slaying of Hrethric.*

[THEN wended the warriors,   bereft of friends, away;
   Back unto their dwellings   in Frisland wended they,
To homes of theirs and high-burg.   But Hengest made his inn,
Still through winter grim and wan,   peacefully with Finn.
His thoughts were of his home-land,   although he might not drive
Over the sea his ringed prow.   Waves with wind did strive;
With storm rolled the ocean;   with ice-fetters fast
Winter locked the billows,—   till there came at last
Another year to homes of men,   as still it doth today—
The glory-gleaming weather   that keeps its times alway.
   Then was gone the winter   and fair was earth's breast;
Forth did fare the rover,—   from Finn's courts, the guest;

Beowulf

But he was thinking rather   of wreaking wrath for wrong,
Than of ocean-voyage: how he might be strong
To bring to pass a battle-parle,   in the which he would
O not all unmindful be   of the Jutemen's brood!
Thus did he refuse not   what is world's behest,
When the son of Hunlaf   had laid upon his breast
The blade hight Battle-Flame,   of all bills the best—
Whose edges to the Jutemen   were known too well.
Likewise to the fierce-heart   Finn in turn befell
The sword-bale bitter   at his very home,
When Guthlaf and Oslaf   o'er the sea did roam,
Bemoaning the sorrow,   the onslaught so grim,
And for a deal of trouble   blaming only him,—
Nor might they in their bold hearts   restrain their restive mood.
Then the hall was reddened   with the foemen's blood;
And King Finn was slaughtered,   'mid his body-corps,
And the queen was taken.   The Scylding bowmen bore
All the wealth in household   of the king of earth—
Whatsoe'er at Finn's home   they could find of worth,
Of gems and wrought jewels—   to their ships away.
On sea-voyage to the Danefolk   the royal wife they bore;
Led her back to kinsmen."]

                    Sung was now the lay,
The harp-chant of gleeman.   Mirth arose once more,
Loud rang the bench-joy.   Cup-bearers did pour
Wine from jars-of-wonder.   Forth came Wealhtheow there,
Walking under golden crown,   to where the friendly pair,
The nephew and the uncle, sate: then was their kinship still at one,
Each unto the other true: And Spokesman Unferth, Ecglaf's son,
Sate at the feet of Scyldings' King.   Both trusted still his spirit bold,
That he was man of courage keen;   though he unto his kin of old
Were not at sword-play merciful.

Beowulf

                        And then the Dame of Scyldings spake:
"Breaker-of-Rings and Free-Lord mine,   now this beaker take;
Be thou blithe of spirit,   thou Gold-Friend in hall;
Bespeak the Geats in happy words,   such as behooves withal;
Be gladsome to the Geatmen,   and not forgetful be
Of good gifts anear or far   which now thou havest free.
'Twas told me, this warrior   thou 'dst take for son to thee.
This bright ring-chamber,   this Heorot, is restored;
Use, while still thou mayest,   thy times for fair reward;
And leave unto thy kinsmen   the folk and the state,
When 't is thine to fare forth,   to greet eternal fate.
I know my gladsome Hrothulf—   that 't is his will to be
Gracious to these boys of ours,   if earlier thou than he,
O thou Friend of Scyldings,   leavest the world behind.
I ween, with goodness he 'll requite   the offspring of us two,
If he all that remembers   that you and I did do
For him when erst a youngling,   with gifts and honors kind."
    Thereat to bench she turned her   where her lads were then,
Hrethric and Hrothmund,   with bairns of fighting men—
The youth all together.   There sate the doughty Thane,
Beowulf, the Geatman,   between the brothers twain.

45

Beowulf

XVIII

THE *Scop chants how Wealhtheow too gave presents to Beowulf, and how one of these presents was a collar which years thereafter Beowulf's Uncle, King Hygelac, wore as he fell in a famous raid down the Frisian Coast. (That was a real raid, historians of the Teutonic tribes assure us; and Hygelac was a real historical personage who lived in the sixth century. Perhaps Beowulf once really lived too; yet I for one doubt if he really did all the big things our Scop tells about him—though it is pleasant and good for us to make-believe he did.) And after Wealhtheow's gifting and speaking, Hrothgar and others, with Beowulf and the Queen too, left the Hall for their rest, leaving behind many jarlmen. These jarlmen took down the feasting boards that had stood on moveable supports in front of the benches along the side walls, and made ready for sleep, unwitting that new terror and woe lurked outside in the night.*

TO HIM she bare the goblet,   and friendly words spake she,
And armlets twain of twisted gold   she proffered graciously,
And rings and a war-coat,   and best of collars too
That ever on earth I heard of.

                  [Nay, I never knew
Under heaven a hero's   treasure goodly more
Since Hama to his bright burg   the Brisings' necklace bore,
With clasp and costly setting.   (He fled the wily mood
Of Eormenric, that angry King,   and chose eternal good.)
This was the very collar   that Hygelac had on,
The Geatman, scion of Swerting,   his last of raids upon,
When he beneath his banner   was fending booty won,
And spoils of war was warding.   Wyrd took him at a stroke,
When in his pride he trouble sought   and feud with Frisian folk.
Yea, he, the mighty Chieftain,   these precious stones had ta'en,
These fair adornments, with him   across the bowl-of-the-main;
And now that he had fallen   beneath his shield at last,

46

Beowulf

His corpse, his mail and collar,   unto the Frankmen passed.
The weaker host was reaving   the spoils of warriors dead
After this battle-hewing;   and this slaughter-stead
The Geatish men were holding.]

                            The hall rang out in glee;
Wealhtheow made a speech then;   before the band spake she:
"Have joy of this collar,   with weal, belovéd Youth!
This war-coat use, my Beowulf—   a royal gift in sooth—
Thrive thou well and show thee   ever strong and free,
And unto these my boys here   kind in counsels be:
For that will I be mindful   of recompense to thee!
Thou hast done so doughtily   that for many a year
Men shall do thee honor   both from far and near,
As widely as the sea-waves   wash each windy wall;
As long as ever thou livest   to thee may good befall!
I wish thee well with treasures!   Unto this my boy
In deeds of thine be helpful,   guarding him his joy!
Here is each jarl to other   true and mild of mood,
Faithful to his Overlord;   all the thanes are good,
The folk at one and ready,   the revelling fighters free.
Do thou as I bid thee."

                     Unto her seat went she.
Here was the best of feastings;   here drank of wine the bold;
They wist not Wyrd was walking,   this grim Fate of old,
Forth for many a jarl there.   When the eve had come
And Hrothgar had hied him   unto his own home—
Unto his rest, the Chieftain—   then did guard the floor
A goodly count of jarlmen   as oft they did before.
The bench-boards they bare off;   and through the hall did strew
The beddings and the bolsters.   And of that boisterous crew
Was one to rest who laid him—   ne'er to wake anew.
At heads they set their bucklers   their war-wood bright.

Beowulf

On bench above each aetheling   there was plain to sight
The steep battle-helmets,   the byrnies of rings,
The spear-shafts sturdy.   For these aethelings
Were wont to be full often   ready for the fray
At home or on a harrying,—   be whichever it may,—
Even on such of seasons   as when befell some stroke
Against their Lord and Master.   That was a doughty folk!

XIX

The Scop chants how Grendel's Mother came that night to the Gold-Ho[ll]
Heorot, and bare off a Danishman and the paw of her dead son Grendel, and ho[w]
on the morrow King Hrothgar grieved anew, just as Beowulf, who knew n[ot]
what had passed, had wended to the King's House to wish Hrothgar a courteo[us]
good morning.

SANK they to sleep then;   was one who purchased sore
His rest there of evening—   as oft had chanced before,
Ever since this Grendel made   Gold-Hall his home,
And wrought there at wrong deeds   till his end did come—
His death after sinnings.   And now 't was seen by men,
And far and wide reported,   that an Avenger then
Yet survived the Monster,—   that all the time Another
Survived this battle-sorrow: Grendel's own Mother,
The She-Thing, the Witch-Wife,   her pang was mourning near,

Beowulf

She who needs must make her   home in grisly mere,
In the cold sea-currents—   after the times when Cain
An only brother, his father's son,   with the sword had slain.
Outlaw, marked for murder,   he fled the joys of folk,
Haunted the wildernesses.   So from him awoke
The breed of fated goblins;   of these was Grendel kin,
That Horror, that Outcast—   who Heorot Hall within
Had found that watchful Human,   awaiting the fight.
There the Ogre gripped him,   but of his strength of might
Beowulf was mindful—   to him God's precious gift—
And trusted the Almighty   for grace and cheer and shift.
Thereby he overcame the Foe;   this Troll of Hell he strook,
Who slunk off acringing,   of his joys forsook,
For to see his death-place—   this Foe of mankind.
    And now his greedy, gloomy   Mother was of mind
To go on quest of sorrow,   to wreak the death of her son.
She came then to Heorot,   where around the floor
The Ring-Danes were sleeping.   Then came to jarls anon
Return of olden evils,   when athrough the door
Burst the Mother of Grendel!   But this was a terror less,
Less by as much as less is   a woman's war-prowéss,
The battling might of maidens,   than a man in fighting dress
(Whenever his falchion, banded,   anvil-beat by the sledge,
His sword with blood bestainéd,   cleaves with its doughty edge
Down through the foeman's boar-crest,   over the helmet's crown).
Then in the hall of Hrothgar,   many a blade was drawn,
Swords from over the benches;   many a buckler tall
Was lifted tight in the hand there!   Never a man in hall
Thought of his helm or corslet—   on whom that fear did fall.
Hers was a sudden hasting—   hers was a turning about
To save her life in the open,   knowing herself found out.
But speedily the Ogress   had seizéd tightly then

Beowulf

One of the Danish house-carls,   as off she fled to fen;
Hrothgar's dearest Hero   in vassal's rank was he,
A mighty shield-warrior,   between the sea and sea,
A fighter of a sure renown   whom in his rest killed she.
And Beowulf was absent,—   for to the Geatman bold
Another lodge allotted was   after the gifts of gold.
Uproar was in Heorot.   Away with her she bore
The famous paw of Grendel,   dripping with its gore.
Sorrow was renewéd   within their homes once more.
'T was an exchange right grievous,   where either side must pay
With the lives of loved ones.
                    Then that Warsman gray,
Old King Hrothgar,   had a heart of pain,
Knowing this Prince was lifeless,   dead this dearest Thane.
Speedily to bower   was Beowulf fetched away,
The victory-blesséd Hero.   And just at dawn of day
He wended with his jarlmen,   this champion Aetheling,
Himself with his comrades,   to where abode the King,
Waiting if All-Wielder   might ever will to show
To him a turn-for-better   after the spell of woe.
Strode along the floor, then,   this Man, the brave-in-brawl,
With his hand-companions,   whilst sounded planks in hall,
To greet with words the Wise One,   and ask the Ingwines' Sire
If he had slept a quiet night   after his desire.

Beowulf

XX

THE *Scop chants how Hrothgar then told Beowulf of the new woe in Heorot* ught *by Grendel's Mother, and of the wild regions of frosted forest and dark* l *where the trollkin dwelt, and of his hope that Beowulf would be again the* ghty *Helper.*

HROTHGAR made a speech then,   Helm of the Scylding-Brood:
  "Nay, ask not after joyance!   Sorrow is renewed
Unto the folk of Daneland.   Dead is now another—
Aescher, of Yrmenlaf   who was the elder brother,
My councillor, my wise-man,   and comrade at my right
Whenever our heads we warded   amidst of the fight,
As clashed the foot-foemen,   and rang the boar-crest—
A jarl should be like Aescher,   an aetheling the best.
Him hath the hand in Heorot   of roving Death-Sprite slain,
And I wot not whither   its backward-ways 't has ta'en,
In its prey exulting,   of its feasting fain.
She hath the feud avengéd   whereby on yester-night
Thou slewest so grimly Grendel   by gripping him so tight—
Because he rent and ravaged   too long my folk in strife.
He fell at last in battle,   paying with his life;
And now hath come another   Scather lorn and lewd,
Who would avenge her offspring—   and farther bears the feud:
So that indeed it seemeth   unto many a thane,
Who weepeth for his Ring-Giver,   a hard heart-bane;
Low lies the hand that wrought ye   your every wish so well.
  I've heard my land-dwellers,   my folk's householders, tell
They'd seen a pair of such ones,   alien Sprites obscure,
Mickle Border-Stalkers,   haunting the moor.
And of these the One was—   as far as guess they might—
The likeness of a woman;   the other wretched Wight

Beowulf

Trod his tracks of exile   in a man's own mien,
Save that he was bigger   than man hath ever been—
Whom the landfolk naméd   Grendel of yore.
Knew they not the father—   whether theretofore
Ever he'd begotten   any troll-kin more.
    Their haunts are secret places,   the wolf-slopes dim,
The headlands windy,   the fen-ways grim,
Where the mountain waterfall   downward away
Floweth under crag-head,   under mists of spray.
And the mere it standeth   off some mile or more:
Over it there hangeth   a forest frosted hoar;
A wood, fast-rooted,   the water over-hoods;
Each night is seen a wonder weird—   a fire on the floods!
There lives no man so wise on earth   whoso its bottom sounds:
Though the heath-ranger,   harried by the hounds,
The hart, strong of antlers,   hunted far in flight,
May seek this woodsy thicket,   he'll rather yield his sprite,
His life upon the brink there,   than plunge for safety in.
A spot uncanny is it;   whence wan to welkin spin
Welter of foam and waters,   when the winds begin
Astirring the foul weather—   till the air is murk,
And the heaven weepeth.
                Again we wait thy work,
Thine and thine only!   That land not yet thou know'st,
The fearsome spot whereunder   thou'lt find that damnéd Ghost—
Seek it, if thou darest!   For this fight to thee
I'll give, as even erst I did,   twisted gold in fee,
Aye, mine olden treasure,   if back thou com'st to me."

Beowulf

XXI

THE *Scop chants Beowulf's confident reply and the journey of Hrothgar, Beo-ulf, and the band along the trail of the Witch-Wife on to the bleak regions, till of sudden along the cliff they came upon the head of the retainer the Witch-Wife ad slaughtered and eaten. And he chants how the waters below were alive with icors and Sea-Serpents, and how Beowulf shot one of them dead with an arrow, d how Beowulf then donned his armor and received from Unferth, who was w a staunch believer in Beowulf, the loan of Unferth's famous sword called runting. (For a sword in those days was so near and dear to a man that it often re a personal name, like a trusted servant.)*

BEOWULF made a speech then,   son of Ecgtheow, he:
"Sorrow not, thou Sage One,—   for each it better be
That his friend he wreaketh   than bemourn him late.
Our end of life in world here   we must all await;
Let who is able win him   glory ere his death;
In after-years for warrior dead   that chiefly profiteth.
Arise thou Kingdom's Warden!   Speedily let us hie
Of this Kin of Grendel   the trail for to spy.
This to thee I promise: She'll refuge in no rest—
Neither in earth's bosom   nor in hill-forést,
Nor in sea-bottom,   wheresoe'er she go!
For this day have patience   in thine every woe,
As I ween thou wilt have."

Beowulf

Upleapt the Graybeard now;
Thanked the Lord Almighty   for what this man did vow.
Then Hrothgar's horse was bridled,   his steed with braided mane;
Stately rode the royal Sage;   and afoot his train
Of shield-bearers was stepping.   Wide was there to see
Her tracks across the wood-ways,   her trail along the lea,
Whither fared she forward   over the murky moor,
And with her bare the dead man,   the best of kin-thanes sure
Of all who once with Hrothgar   warded well the home.
Then the Son of aethelings   now did over-roam
The narrow-passes,   the steep cliff-stone,
The close defiles and   the paths unknown,
The beetling cragheads,   the Nicors' den.
All ahead he hastened with   a few wise men
For to view the region,   till a sudden he
Found the joyless forest,   found the mountain tree,
Leaning o'er the hoar cliff.   Under the wood,
Blood-stained and troubled,   there the waters stood.
Unto the friends of Scyldings,   unto every Dane,
It was a thing of sorrow,   a burden of heart's pain,
Aye, to many a clansman   a grief it was and dread,
When, upon the sea-cliff,   they met with Aescher's head!

   The flood with blood was boiling,   yes, with the hot gore;
The folk saw down upon it;   the horn was singing o'er
Its battle-blast of onset.   The band all sate;
They watched along the water   the sea-worms great,
Monsters of the dragon-breed,   trying there the sea,
And on the foreland ledges   Nicors lying free
(Who're wont at early morning   their grievous quest to take
Out upon the sail-road)—   and wild-beast and snake.
Bitter and puffed with anger,   they hastened away—
They had heard that clangor,   the war-horn's lay.

Beowulf

One did the Geatish Leader   with arrow-bow from shore
Berob of life forever   and of the waves' uproar.
The warrior-shaft, the hardy,   unto his heart went home—
He whom death had taken swam   more sluggish on the foam!
Speedily on the billows   with barbed boar-spears
They pressed him so sorely,   they harried him so fierce,
And dragged him up the ledges,   this wave-tossing Ranger.
The marvelling warriors looked upon   the grim and grisly Stranger.
    Girded himself, did Beowulf,   with his jarlman's weeds;
Naught for his life he mournéd.   His coat of mail must needs,
Bright with deft devices,   be trying the sea-quest—
This hand-woven byrnie big,   that girt his bony-chest,
So never a grip-in-battle   might do his bosom scath,
Nor life be hurt by vengeful grasp   of this Thing-of-Wrath.
The head of him was guarded   by the helmet white
That soon must seek the sounding surge   and stir the deeps below:
With lordly bands 't was bounden,   with treasure-work 't was dight,
As the weapon-smith had wrought it   in days of long ago,
And wondrously had decked it   and set with shapes of boar,
That brand nor blade of battle   might bite it nevermore.
    Nor was that the smallest   of helps to mighty deed
Which Spokesman of Hrothgar   had loaned him in his need:
A good sword hafted,   and Hrunting its name,
Of all old heirlooms   the first it was in fame.
The edge of it was iron,   etched with twig and spray,
Hardened by the battle-blood;   ne'er did it betray
Any man that clasped it   with hand amid the fray,—
Any man that dared to go   on war-paths away,
To folk-stead of foemen.   Nor this the first time now
That Hrunting-sword of Unferth   in mighty works should dow.
In sooth the bairn of Ecglaf,   great though his prowess be,
Remembered not his speech of late   when drunk with wine was he,—

Beowulf

Now as he lent his weapon   to a stouter swordsman here.
Himself he durst not hazard   his own life in the mere,
Nor dree a warrior's duty.   And thus he lost the fame,
The glory of a doughty deed.   For the Other 't was not so,
When he himself had girded   for battle with the Foe.

XXII

THE *Scop chants Beowulf's parting speech to Hrothgar, in which Beowulf now acknowledges gratefully Hrothgar's adoption of him as son and repays Unferth's generosity for the loan of Hrunting by willing Unferth his own sword should he not return alive from battle with Grendel's Dam. The Scop chants Beowulf's descent under the sea and the perilous beginning of the fight, and how Beowulf soon found himself in a deep-sea hall where no water was; how Hrunting failed him at the stroke, and how Beowulf, relying again on sheer strength, stumbled and fell so that the Mere-Woman squatted upon him and drew her dirk. The Scop chants that Beowulf's stout armor and God's good help saved him awhile. Did they save him to the end?*

BEOWULF made his speech then,   bairn of Ecgtheow, he:
"Bethink thee now, thou mighty   son of Halfdane's name,
Gold-Friend of house-carls,   Sovran wise and free,
Bethink thee, now I 'm girt for quest,   what we twain spake before:
If for thy need, O Hrothgar,   my life I should give o'er,
That thou to me wouldst ever be,   when I 'm no longer here,

56

Beowulf

Still in the place of a father;   every trusty fere,
Each of these my kin-thanes,   do thou as guardian tend,
If once the battle take me;   and likewise, O my Friend,
These treasures that thou gavest me   unto my Master send.
Then Hyglac, son of Hrethel,   may ken from all this gold,
Aye, see, when he beholdeth   these giftings rich and old,
That I indeed had found me   a Treasure-Giver bright,
And had my joy in him and his   so long as still I might.
And let thou, too, thy Unferth,   that far-famed soul,
Have the olden heirloom,   the sword with wavy scroll,
Hard of edge and jewelled.   In Hrunting will I trust
To work my doom of glory—   or I die the death I must."

    After these his words the Geat,   Beowulf, in pride
Hastened in his valor.   No answer would he bide.
The billows took the Battle-Man.   'Twas a while of the day
Ere he arrived the sea-floor   where the Monster lay.
And soon this grim and greedy   She-Thing ravin-fierce,
That held the stretches of the floods   a hundred half-years,
Found that there some one of men   from up above had sought
The dwelling-place of eldritch-wights.   Against him then she caught,
With grisly claws she gripped him.   His warrior-body sound
Thereby no whit she scathéd.   His mail did shield him round
So that reach she might not,   with loathly fingers stark,
Athrough his army-corslet,   his linkéd battle-sark.
Then as she to the bottom came,   this She-Wolf of the sea,
She bore unto her own home   the Chieftain-of-the-Rings,
In such a wise he might not,   albeit so wroth was he,
Ever wield his weapons.   And many monstrous Things
Mauled him in the maelstrom,   many a sea-beast tried,
With its battling tushes,   to burst his sark aside,
And swarmed upon their Troubler.   Then was the Jarl aware
That he was in some hall of hate—   he knew not what or where—

Beowulf

In which not any water   could scathe him at all,
Nor floods in onrush touch him   because of rooféd hall;
And he saw a light of fire,   a brightly flashing flare.
And Beowulf had a look then   upon this deep-sea Troll,
This mighty Mere-Woman.   Then up with sword and soul
He made a sudden onset,   nor hand delayed the stroke,
And on her head the ringéd blade   its greedy war-song woke.
But, lo, the Stranger found then   his flasher-in-the-fray
Would bite not, would scathe not   the life it sought today,
For Hrunting's edge was failing   the Chief in his distress,
Though often in the old days   it had endured the press,
And cloven many a helmet,   and war-coat of the fey:
This was the first of all times   that low its glory lay.
Again had he but one thought,—   nor courage did he lack,—
Still mindful of valor,   this Kin of Hygelac!
In wrath the Champion hurléd   the fretted blade away,
Bound on hilt with ring-work,   till there on earth it lay,
That stout sword and steel-edged;   and on main strength relied,
The might of his old hand-grip.   So must a man of pride,
Whenever he bethinks him   to win in battle-strife
Praises everlasting,   nor careth for his life.
The Chieftain of the Geatfolk,—   who mourned not at the feud,—
Graspéd by her mane of hair   Grendel's Mother lewd.
This hardy son of battle,—   so did his anger swell,—
Flung the deadly She-Wolf   till to ground she fell.
Speedily thereafter,   with her grip so grim,
She gave him goodly payment   and laid her hold on him.
And then with heart aweary,   this Fighter fierce and lone
Stumbled in his footing,   that there he tumbled prone.
Then on the Stranger in her hall   The Mother squatted down,
And forth she drew her dagger,   broad of blade and brown.
She would wreak her bairn now,   her only child this day;

Beowulf

But on the Geatman's shoulders⠀⠀the woven breast-mail lay,
And that withstood the inthrust⠀⠀of point and edge at last.
For then the son of Ecgtheow⠀⠀to under-earth had passed,
Had not his battle-byrnie,⠀⠀his war-mesh stout and broad,
To him its help y-given,⠀⠀and had not holy God,
The Ruler, he, of Heaven,⠀⠀justly swayed the fight—
The wise Lord with his award—⠀⠀when Beowulf stood upright.

XXIII

THE *Scop twangs his harp to words more stirring still, chanting how Beowulf found an old sword in the hall of the Mere-Wife and smote her dead on the neck-bone, and how there by a mysterious sudden light he saw Grendel's cadaver and cut off Grendel's head and how the blade melted; how then Hrothgar and the Danes on the cliffs above saw the waters all bloody and thought Beowulf must have perished and so went home, while still Beowulf's little band remained gloomily behind; how Beowulf swam up to the surface with the hilt of the sword and with Grendel's head; and how Beowulf with his little band of Geatmen marched in triumph back to Heorot with Grendel's head dangling by hair from a spear-shaft borne on the shoulders of four.*

FOR saw he 'mongst the war-gear⠀⠀one victorious bill,
An old sword of ettins,⠀⠀with edges doughty still,
The pick and choice of weapons,⠀⠀a warsman's prize indeed;
But more than any other man⠀⠀might bear in battle-need—

Beowulf

Good and brave to look on,   the giants' handicraft.
The Bold One of the Scyldings   he seized its belted haft;
And, battle-grim and savage,   the ringéd blade he drew;
And, of his life all hopeless,   in fury smote so true
That it gripped her sorely   unto the neck, oho!
And brake in twain its bone-rings.   The sword was keen to go
Athrough her dooméd body.   She crumpled in the murk.
The old sword was bloody.   The Hero liked his work.
     And the gleam out-blazéd,   within there stood a light,
As from heaven shineth   the sky's Candle bright.
He looked about the dwelling,   he turned him to the wall,
He heaved by hilt the weapon,   this hardiest sword of all;
Wroth and with but *one* thought,   the Thane of Hygelac—
With its edge not useless   for such a man's attack!—
Speedily was of a will   to pay that Grendel back
For his many onslaughts   made on folk West-Dane,
Mickle more than one time,   when asleep he'd slain
Hrothgar's hearth-fellows,   and slumbering eat with jaws
Fifteen of Danish folk   and fifteen borne in claws
Outward, his ghastly prey.   For Beowulf, the dread,
Paid him his award for that,   where he beheld on bed
Grendel, the battle-weary,   lying lorn of life,
Ev'n by scathe he'd gotten   in Heorot at the strife.
The corse did spring asunder;   it dreed a blow, though dead,
Oho, a swinging war-stroke,—   and off was carved the head!
     The wise carls that with Hrothgar   sate peering at the flood
Soon saw the surges swirling,   the sea all stained with blood.
The white-haired ones together   about the brave Man speak:
Saying they ween the Aetheling   no more will come to seek,
In the pride of victory,   their glorious Overlord,
Since him it seemed to many   the Sea-Wolf had devoured.
Then came the day's ninth hour;   the Scyldings left the ness;

Beowulf

The Gold-Friend of clansman,   Hrothgar, hied him home;
Only the Geatish strangers   sate in their distress,
Sick at heart with longing,   and stared upon the foam.
They wished but never weened to see   their dear Lord's self again.
   Then the sword, the war-bill,   'gan wondrously to wane
In icicles of battle,   by goblin-gore accurst:
Likest to ice it melted,   when God, the Father, first
The bands of frost doth loosen,   unfettering stream and pool,—
He's Lord of times and seasons,   and very sooth his rule!
The Chieftain of the Weder-Geats   he took not from the lair
Not any goods of treasure   (though saw he many there),
Except the head of Grendel   and hilt so bravely dight:
The fretted blade had burnt away,   the sword had melted quite—
So hot had been the blood of her,   so poison-fierce withal
Had been this eldritch Ogress   that died there in the hall.
But he who in the combat   did bide the demon-slaughter
Soon was at his swimming,   up-diving through the water.
   Cleansed were surge and stretches wide,   where the grim Mere-Wife
Had left this fleeting world of ours   and her days of life.
The sea-farer's Safe-guard,   this Stout-Heart of toil,
Came striking out to landward,   fain of his sea-spoil,
Fain of his booty-burden.   Went to meet him then
His staunch troop of tribesmen,   thanked the God of men,
Rejoiced in him their Leader   to see him sound again.
Helm and mail of Hero   they loosened with a will;
The waters under welkin,   the bloody pool, was still;
Forth they fared in foot-prints,   these happy aethelings;
The earth-way, the known road,   they measured, bold as kings.
They bare the head from sea-cliff,   a load for each, though stout,
And four upon the spear-pole   scarce lifted it about
Onward to the Gold-Hall,   till into hall bedene
They came, these brave-in-battle,   these Geatmen, the fourteen.

Beowulf

Their Chieftain in a mighty mood   amid them trod the mead,
Till he, as first of clansmen,   this Man so keen of deed,
Hero, battle-hardy,   with glory honoréd,
Came to greet his Hrothgar.   And now is Grendel's head
Borne by hair where warriors drink,—   to jarls and Lady there
A gruesome vision wondrous.   The Danes upon it stare.

XXIV

THE *Scop chants Beowulf's account to Hrothgar of the deep-sea fight, and how Beowulf presented him with the hilt of the deep-sea sword; how Hrothgar gazed on that hilt whereon was graven in runic staves the Bible story of the flood (for our Anglo-Saxon forefathers combined in their imagination stories of their old heathen days with Christian stories told by Monks and Abbots). And the Scop chants the beginning of Hrothgar's long speech to Beowulf, so full of an old man's wisdom and advice, in which Hrothgar to his sound precepts added the profitable example of the evil career and evil end of a former Danish King, Heremod, who reigned cruelly before the coming of Scyld.*

BEOWULF made his speech then,   son of Ecgtheow, he:
  "Lo, thou Son of Halfdane,   with joy we've brought to thee,
As token of glory,   this spoil thou here dost see,
O Sovran of the Scyldings.   I barely 'scaped with life;
Unsoftly did I risk the work   in under-water strife;

Beowulf

Straight had the battle ended,   had God not been my shield,
For Hrunting in the combat   I might in no wise wield,
Though doughty be that weapon.   But he, mankind's Defender,
Gave me upon the wall to see,   hanging in its splendor,
A huge sword of old times.   (Oft and oft withal
The Father guides the friendless.)   I drew that sword from wall,
Then slew I at the onset,   when my chance was good,
The Wardens of that under-house.   But so sprang the blood,
The hottest gore of slaughter,   that the fretted blade,
The battle-bill, was burnt all.   From my foes I made,
Bearing thence the hilt away.   I wreaked the crimes of hell,
The death-fall of Danishmen,   as was fit and well.
I promise thee in Heorot   a sleep care-free,
With band of thy retainers,   each who follows thee,
Of the older, of the younger;   and ever from that quarter,
O Sovran of the Scyldings,   release from dread of slaughter
For these here, thy jarlmen,   as erst 't was thine to dree."
   Then was that hilt, the golden,   the giants' work of yore,
Giv'n to hand of the old King,   the Battle-Leader hoar;
After the fall of devils,   to Hrothgar's keep it fell—
This work of wonder-smithmen;   yea, when this Heart-of-Hell,
God's Foeman, murder-guilty,   this world of ours gave o'er
(And eke this Grendel's Mother),   it passed into the power
Of him, the best of World-Kings   of all between the seas
Who e'er on Scandia's island dealt   men their golden fees.
   Hrothgar made his speech then;   on hilt he cast his eyes,
Relic of the olden time,   whereon was writ the rise
Of that far-off warfare,   when o'erwhelmed the flood
And the ocean's outpour   once the giants' brood:
They bore themselves too boldly,   a folk estranged from God;
For this the Lord made end-award   by whelming under wave.
So on the golden sword-guard,   in many a runic stave,

Beowulf

Was marked aright and set and said   for whom was wrought of yo
That best of steel with twinéd hilt,   and etched with dragons o'er.
     Then spake wise Son of Halfdane—   and still were all the throng
"Lo, one, like me, who's warded   a kingdom long and long,
And for his folk still worketh   the right and the sooth,
One who remembers all of old,   may say this thing indeed:
That here's a very jarlman   born of better breed.
Thy fame shall be uplifted,   my belovéd youth,
Among all peoples, Beowulf,   over the wide ways;
And thou shalt hold thy prowess   with wisdom all thy days;
My troth to thee will I fulfill,   e'en as we spake before.
Thou'lt be unto thy people   an aid forevermore,
A help unto the heroes.
                          Not so was Heremod
Unto Ecgwela's children,   the Scylding-folk, the good.
Nor waxed he to their pleasure,   but unto every Dane
Was he the dire undoing   and the deadly bane.
In wrath of heart he slew those   who drank with him and ate
And stood beside his shoulders,   till he, the King so great,
Lonely passed from cheer of men.   Yet God advancéd him
And raised in power, in joys of strength,   above all human kin.
His hoard of thoughts in bosom,   however, bloodier grew;
He gave no rings to Danefolk,   as kings are wont to do.
Lorn of joy he bided;   the work of strife he dreed,
The long feud of his people.
                                    Learn from this thy rede;
Know what is manly virtue.   As one in winters gray,
For thee I've told this story.   A wonder 't is to say
How mighty God on men bestows,   in his forethought free,
Wisdom, lands, and earlship.   All things ruleth he:
Whiles letteth he the heart-thought   of man of noble birth
In lustihead go faring,   giveth joy of earth,

Beowulf

Giveth in his native land   a walled burg to keep,
Granteth stretches of the world,   realms so wide of sweep,
That he himself the ends thereof   may ween not in his thought.
Dwelleth he in fatness;   him thwarteth never aught
Of either eld or sickness;   nor any evil care
Beclouds in murk his spirit;   nor feuding anywhere,
With sword and hatred, threatens.   Unto his will and lot
All the world is wending.   The worse he knoweth not. . . .

XXV

THE *Scop continues to chant Hrothgar's Sermon to Beowulf, from which I hope we may profit as much as Beowulf surely did. Then he chants how, after a night of more feasting and some sleep, the Geatish Visitors with the morning sun made ready to fare back to Geatland.*

TILL wakes and waxeth in him   pride, a mickle deal;
Whilst the Watchman sleepeth,   the Warden of souls' weal—
Aye, very fast that sleeping,   and bound with busy woe,
The Slayer very nigh him   who shoots from grievous bow.
Then is he in his bosom,   under helmet hit
By a bitter arrow—   he knoweth not a whit
How he now may shield him   from wonder-spells of wrong
Of the curséd Demon.   What he held so long

Beowulf

He thinketh now too little.   Greedy, grim, and bold,
He never gives with goodly boast   the rings of plated gold;
Forgetteth he and spurneth   the fate that comes to all,
Because the King-of-Glory   him gave such good of old.
But in the end it happens   his fleeting frame doth fall,—
Death-marked it sinketh.   Another now succeeds,
Who gladly deals that jarl's old wealth   and spurneth ugly deeds.
   Best of men, dear Beowulf,   keep from bale and feud;
Choose for thyself the better part,   the everlasting good.
Spurn, renownéd Fighter,   over-much of pride;
Now shall thy fame in valor   a little while abide:
Soon shall be hereafter,   that sickness or the glaive
Part thee from thy prowess—   or the whelming wave,
Or the fang of fire,   or the flight of spears,
Or the grip of falchion,   or the aging years;
Or else thine eyes' brightness   shall fail and darkened be,
And death anon, O Warrior-Son,   shall over-master thee.
   Half a hundred winters,   under the welkin, lo,
I held my sway o'er Ring-Danes,   and warded them in war
With ash-stock and steel-edge,   'gainst clans anear and far,
So well that I did count me   'neath all the skies no foe.
Behold! a change there came to me   then in my father's home—
Grief instead of good times,   when Grendel did become,
He, the olden Enemy,   invader of my floor;
Ever for his raidings   mickle care I bore.
Thanks to God eternal,   that I did bide in life
Long enough with eyes to see,   after olden strife,
That head from sword so gory.   Go, now, to thy seat;
Enjoy the merry feasting, thou,   honored by thy feat.
Many a gift between us twain   there'll be upon the morrow."
   Went to seek his seat then,   the Geat so free of sorrow,
As the Wise One bade him.   And now, as erst, again

Beowulf

The feast was dight so fairly   for valor-famous men,
The sitters in that hall-house. . . .   The helmet of the night
Darkened dusky o'er the band.   Arose each warrior-wight;
The hoary agéd Scylding   was fain to seek his bed;
The Geat did list him passing well   to lay to rest his head,
He, the famous Shieldman.   And soon the Thane-in-hall—
Who tended with meet courtesy   the Hero's needments all
(Ev'n as these ocean-farers   were worthy of the best)—
Led forth the Hero come from far,   weary from his quest.
So rested he, the Great-Heart.   That House it towered high,
Broad-roofed, gold-bright.   Within it slept the guest,
Until the black raven   with his blithesome cry
Boded the Joy-of-Heaven.   Onward came the Bright,
The Shine that follows shadow.   Hastened every wight;
Aethelings were eager   back to folk to fare;
The Big-Heart would take ship   far away from there.
Bade he then, this Brave One,   Unferth Hrunting bear,
Bade him take his sword again,   the iron blade so lief;
Thanked him for the loan thereof;   quoth, he counted it
A friend-in-war, a good and great;   belied he not a whit
The edge of Unferth's falchion.   That was a gallant chief!
And when the braves were forward,   ready in their gear,
Then stepped he forth, the Hero,   he to Danes so dear,
To where was there the Other   high on kingly seat,
And then this battling Aetheling   did his Hrothgar greet.

Beowulf

XXVI

THE Scop chants Beowulf's courteous farewell to Hrothgar, and Hrothgar's farewell to Beowulf in which Hrothgar prophesied that Beowulf would some day succeed Hygelac as King of the Geats. And the Geatmen marched off to their Ship on the coast.

BEOWULF made his speech then,   son of Ecgtheow, he:
"Lo, we far-comers,   we farers on the sea,
Have a will to say now   we'd seek our Hygelac.
Thou hast been a goodly host;   in nothing did we lack.
O Lord of men, if ever   I may this earth upon
Earn me of thy heart's love   more than yet I've done,
By aught of work-of-battle,   I'll ready be anon.
If across the long seas,   ever I should hear
That the dwellers round about   burden thee with fear,
As the haters of thy realm   have done of yester-year,
I'll bring to thee a thousand thanes,   braves for help to thee.
I wot me of my Hygelac,   though so young he be,
This Sovran of us Geatmen,   this Herdsman of our ledes,
That he will well uphold me   both by words and deeds,
That I may do thee honor,   and to thy succor bear
Ashen spear and aid of might,   if need of men be there.
If, too, thy Hrethric,   bairn of kingly birth,
Betakes him to the Geatish court,   he'll find of friends no dearth:
'T is good to see a far countree,   for one who trusts his worth."
Hrothgar made his speech then,   answering him anon:
"The wise God these sayings sent   into thy soul, my son.
Ne'er heard I more sagely   so young a man take part;
Strong in might, and sound in thought,   and wise in words thou art.
Most likely do I count it,   if haply spear take him,
The offspring of Hrethel,   in battle bloody-grim,—
If illness, aye, or iron,   take him to whom ye vow,

Beowulf

This Herdsman of your people,— and if alive art thou,
That then the Sea-Geats cannot make seemlier choice for King,
For Hoard-Ward of heroes, than thou, my Aetheling,
If then thou 'rt not unwilling thy kindred's realm to hold.
Me liketh thy brave spirit, belovéd Friend and bold,
The longer the better. Beowulf, 't was thine
To bring to pass between us, between thy folk and mine,
The Geat-clan, the Spear-Danes, that common peace shall be,
And strife shall rest, the ugly feuds, which both erewhile did dree;
That there shall be, as long as I rule this Kingdom wide,
Treasures in common, and greetings either side,
Gifts the one to other over the gannet's bath;
And that the ringéd ship shall bring over the ocean path
Offering and love-token. I wot our peoples hold,
Knit as one, to friend and foe, all blameless as of old."
　Thereto the Son of Halfdane, whom 'Shield of jarls' they call,
To Beowulf presented treasures twelve in hall.
And bade him with these giftings his own, his dear domain
To seek in weal and safety, and quickly come again.
And then the Lord of Scyldings, the King of birth so high,
Kissed the best of aethelings and clasped his neck thereby;
The tears they were afalling from him, the old man hoar;—
Two likelihoods he thought of— but one of them the more:
That never thereafter might they each other scan,
Proud men in parley. So lief was him this man
That now his breast's upheaving seemed too much to bear;
Bound within his bosom a secret longing there
After the man belovéd burned into his blood.
　But Beowulf thence away the grass-plain trod,
War-man, gold-proud, fain of treasure-fee.
There at anchor riding, a goer-on-the-sea
Was its master biding. And marching to the main,

Beowulf

The Geatmen spoke of Hrothgar's boon   again and yet again.
That was a King all spotless . . .   till from his joys of strength
Eld, that scathes so many men,   took him too at length.

XXVII

The *Scop chants how the Coast Guard, who had challenged Beowulf s*
sternly when he had landed on the Danish Shore, now rode to meet him in wel
coming wise, and how Beowulf gave to the Dane who had guarded his craft
golden sword; how the craft, laden with treasures (armor and horses), spe
over the sea under sail in a fair brisk wind, and how Beowulf and his band wer
met on the home-shore by the Haven Guard who had long been watching fo
their return, and how they saw Hygelac's castle not far away.   And here th
Scop is reminded of Hygelac's young queen Hygd in the castle, and, while we ar
impatient to have him chant how Beowulf reported his adventure to his King
our Scop makes a curious and annoying digression, chanting the cruelties of an
other royal lady (contrasted with the admirable Hygd, as cruel King Heremo
had been contrasted with Beowulf).   This lady was named Thryth, and she ha
the very wicked habit of causing every man who gazed upon her eyes (pre
sumably as a wooer) to be put to death, until a certain bold Prince, called Off
managed to become her husband,—when, lo, ever afterwards she was docile an
genial enough.

So CAME the press of henchmen,   these bold ones, to the bark;
Each bare his ringéd harness,   the linkéd battle-sark.
The Land Guard, as erst, spied   the jarls again on quest;

Beowulf

But not with any words of harm,   from the headland's crest,
Greeted he the strangers.   Toward he rode with hail;
Welcomed, as the scathers fared   to ship in shining mail.
Then on the sand was laden   the boat of bulwarks wide,—
The ringéd craft was laden   with armor side by side,
With horses and with treasures.   The mast aloft it soared
Over Hrothgar's olden   piléd treasure-hoard.
Beowulf gave the Boat Guard   a gold-bound sword;
And ever thereafter   upon the mead-bench he
Was worthier for that heirloom   that gift from o'er the sea.
   The craft it clave deep water;   from Daneland far it passed,
Upon the mast a sea-cloth,   a sail by rope made fast;
Groaned and creaked the sea-wood;   the wind it never drave
From off its billowy course there   that bounder-on-the-wave;
Foamy-necked it floated   over the billows free,
Over the streams of ocean,   that goer-on-the-sea—
Until the cliffs of Geatland   the sailors sighted plain,
The old familiar nesses.   The keel upsprang amain,
Speeded by the wildwinds,   and rested on the land.
   The Haven Guard was straightway   helping at the strand,
He who long already,   eager by the mere,
Had been awatching far-off   for the men so dear.
He bound that boat of bosom broad   with anchor-cordage fast,
Lest this their merry vessel   the waves away should cast;
Then Beowulf bade bear out   the wealth of aethelings,
The plated gold and trappings.   Not far from here it is

To seek the son of Hrethel,   Giver-of-the-Rings,
Where at home he dwelleth,   himself with comrades his,—
Hyglac near the sea-wall.   That house was very fair;
Its lord a King renownéd,   the halls were lofty there;
And Hygd, of Haereth daughter,   was young, but well-beseen,

Beowulf

Albeit so few her winters   within the burg as queen—
Aye, none the less no chary,   no niggard lady she
Unto the Geats with giftings,   but one with treasures free.

[Hygd, the goodly Folk-Queen,   showed not the mood of Thryth,
Nor Thryth's misdeeds of terror.   Was none of kin and kith
So brave, he durst adventure   with eyes to face her eyes
(Except her husband only).   For well would he surmise
Bonds of death would ready be,   a hand-twisted cord;
And hard upon his seizure   she'd summon her the sword,
For scrolléd blade to settle it,   and thus his death reveal.
'T is not a queenly custom,   for woman so to deal,
E'en though she be so fair of face,   aye, such a man to kill
(She who's called 'Peace-Weaver'),   in fury for no ill.
But Hemming's kinsman verily   did end her ruthless pride,
And men amid their ale-drinking   often said beside
That less she wrought of folk-bale,   and less all mercy scorned,
So soon as she was given,   she, the gold-adorned,
Unto the youthful Fighter,   the high-born and good,
When at her father's bidding   she voyaged o'er the flood,
Unto the hall of Offa;   where after on the throne
All her life she loved her lot,   with a fair renown;
And fostered a deep fondness   toward this Prince of thanes—
The best, as some have told me,   in all the wide domains,
Of all the race of mankind,   that dwell the seas between;
And therefore this Offa,   this Man spear-keen,
Widely was honored   for wars and gifts of hand;
With wisdom he ruléd   his own home-land.
And unto him was born, then,   Eomaer, a son—
Grandson of Garmund,   of Hemming's kinsman one,
A mighty man in battle,   a help to every band.]

Beowulf

XXVIII-XXIX (XXX?)

(THE Scribe who wrote down the Scop's song seems to have made a mistake
dividing these two 'fyttes,' as such chapters of old stories in verse used to be
*lled; so they are treated here as one. And, moreover, he numbers the next fytte
XXXI, omitting division XXX. I should say either 'XXXI' is the Scribe's mis-
*ke for 'XXX' or XXX was originally the latter part of what the Scribe includes
XXIX. Learned men in their lecture-rooms in Universities spend much time
discussing such problems as this.)

The Scop chants Beowulf's coming to Hygelac, Hygelac's eager questions to
*eowulf, and Beowulf's long account of those adventures of which you and I
*ve already heard. A skilful modern story-teller would avoid such a repetition;
*ut in the old days the Scops had different notions about what was artistic, and
*rought with their own skill in their craft. And indeed, are we not pleased to
*ar just how Beowulf himself felt about his deeds, especially as he adds some new
*tails about Hrothgar, his host? Are we not imaginatively present there with
*ygelac, who did not know what had passed since Beowulf fared away? But
*e Scop makes Beowulf indulge in a long digression about the marriage of
*reawaru, the daughter of his Danish host Hrothgar, with Ingeld, prince of the
*eathobards; and you and I may well feel like taking the Scop to task for break-
*g the narrative flow and for having Beowulf talk about things that under the
*rticular circumstances it is unlikely either he or Hygelac would have been
*inking of at all. And, too, he makes Beowulf specify some future events,
*hich were long past by the time the Scop chanted, but could not have been
*reseen by Beowulf, unless we imagine he was a Wizard and Prophet as well as a

73

Beowulf

*Strong Man—and perhaps he was, after all.   However, the story of Freawaru
and Ingeld was itself once very famous.   It seems that Hrothgar had brought
about the alliance in order to end a long strife between Danes and Heathobards;
but that, when the lady entered the court of the Heathobards, she was accompanied by a Danish warrior foolishly wearing a sword originally taken in battle
from a Heathobard warrior, and this insult speedily put an end to the peace.   In
the war that followed, it appears, according to legends not recited by our Scop,
that Heorot Hall was set on fire and destroyed.*

'GAN then the Hardy One,   himself along the sand,
  To tread upon the sea-plains,   the stretches of the strand,
With his feres, the trusty.   The world's Candle shone,
The Spangle risen southward.   They strode along alone;
Sturdily they marchéd,   to where they heard that now
Hygelac, the Shield of jarls,   slayer of Ongentheow,
Within the burg was dealing   ring upon ring,—
Hygelac, the good, he,   the young War-King.
The coming-back of Beowulf   to him was quickly told,
How thither to the King's house   this Shield of battlers bold,
And of the buckler-bearers,   was coming on his way
Alive unto the court there,   safe from battle-play.
    Anon, as then the Sovran bade,   the hall within was dight
For these guests, these way-farers.   And he who fought the fight
Sate him by the King's self,   kin his kin beside,
After he had greeted   in courtesy and pride
His Liege-Lord, the gracious.   With mead-draughts for all,
Hygd, of Haereth daughter,   went round about the hall.
She lovéd these the people;   she bare for the carouse
The stoup to hands of Geatmen.   In high hall-house
Hygelac in fair wise   questionings addressed
To Beowulf, his house-carl;   with longing burst his breast
To hear how well his Sea-Geats   had thriven on their quest.

74

Beowulf

"Dear Beowulf, what luck, then,   upon this voyage, for thee,
After thou bethoughtest,   over the salt-sea,
To seek afar the battle,   and strife at Heorot?
For Hrothgar, the great King,   hast bettered now or not
That woe so widely told of?   For this I seethed in breast
With care and surging sorrow.   Me liked not such a quest
For man so much belovéd.   And long I begged of thee
That thou that eldritch Ogre   would let forever be,
And let themselves the South-Danes   settle as they may
The warfare with Grendel.   To God my thanks I say
That I can look upon thee   sound again today."
   Beowulf made his speech then,   bairn of Ecgtheow, he:
"O that is no wise hidden   from men, where'er they be,
That our famous meeting,   Hygelac, my lord,—
How on that very field there   I and Grendel warred
Where he so oft and often   had wrought the sorrow-stroke
And miseries forever   on Victor-Scylding folk.
All that so well I vengéd   that none of Grendel's kin,
None on earth that longest   lives begirt by sin,
Of this breed, the loathsome,   will care to boast withal
Of the din there in the dawning.
                    But unto the ring-hall
First did I betake me   Hrothgar to greet;
Soon when he, the mighty   Child of Halfdane,
Knew the thought within me,   he yielded me a seat
There beside his own son.   Thane rejoiced with thane;
I never saw in all my life,   under the heavens all,
More merriment at mead among   sitters in a hall.
Whiles the Queen, the high-born,   whom 'Peace-Bringer' they call,
Passed, as she cheered the younger braves,   around through all the hall,
And gave to many a warrior,   rings of wreathéd gold,
Ere yet she went unto her seat.   And whiles unto the old,

Beowulf

To every jarl, the ale-stoup   did Hrothgar's daughter bear—
She whom I heard the sitters   within the hall-house there,
As she the bosséd beaker gave,   Freawaru name.

[Betrothed is Freawaru,   the young, the golden dame,
To the glad son of Froda.   For Hrothgar did devise,
He, the Kingdom's Shepherd,   a rede he counted wise:
Even through her, this Lady,   to set old feuds at rest,
And end a deal of slaughter.   But seldom 't is at best,
After a prince's death-fall,   that spears are laid aside,
More than for a little while—   however fair the bride.
And Ingeld may not like it,   nor any of his thanes,
When there shall pace adown his hall   a courtier of the Danes,
Leading in this Lady   past many a Heathobard,
And shining with the heirloom,   the fretted sword and hard—
The Heathobards' treasure,   what time they wielded stroke,
Until they lost at linden-play   their lives and fellow-folk.
And then shall some old spearsman,   who marks the precious thing,
Grimly o'er the ale-cup   speak remembering
The tribesmen pierced and fallen,   and 'gin in grief of breast
To stir some stripling's bosom,   his fighting soul to test,
To wake in him the war-hate.   And this the word he saith:
   'Canst thou not, my comrade,   ken the sword of death,
Which to the fray thy father bore   upon his final quest
Under his casque-of-battle,—   this blade of iron dear,—
Where the Danemen slew him,   and Scyldings bold-with-spear
Held the field of slaughter,   victors over all,
When Withergild lay lifeless   after our heroes' fall!
Lo, now some upstart youngling   from out these men-of-bane,
Proud of these his trappings,   paces down the hall,
Vaunteth of that murder,   and doth that jewel bear
The which by right, my comrade,   thou alone shouldst wear.'

Beowulf

So urgeth he and eggeth   again and yet again
With words sore and bitter;   till good time succeeds
When the Lady's serving Thane   for his father's deeds,
After the bite of battle-bill,   sleepeth and bleeds,
With his life a forfeit.   The venger fleeth thence;
And living he escapeth,   for well the land he kens.
The sworn oaths of jarlmen   are broken on each side;
And welleth feud in Ingeld,   and all his love of bride,
In surgings of his sorrows,   waxeth cooler now.
Therefore I count the Heathobards'   peace pact and vow
Guileful to Danishmen,   their friendship not fast.]

But once again of Grendel   I must speak at last,
That thou, O Treasure-Giver,   may know the end aright
Of the hand-fray of the heroes.   When heaven's Jewel bright
Had glided from the fields of earth,   came that angry Sprite,
The grisly Evening-Goblin,   for to seek us out,
Where we the hall were warding,   Geatmen stout.
And then was unto Handscio   the warfare come amain,
Bale to him, the fey man.   'T was he that first was slain,
He, the girded Fighter.   Our kindred's mighty Thane
Died in the mouth of Grendel.   Grendel swallowed him,
The body of that dear man,   head and trunk and limb.
Yet not for this the sooner   would he quit withal,
He, the Slayer bloody-toothed,   the gold-decked hall,
Still mindful of murders,   still empty-handed, he!
But, terrible in prowess,   did he try for me,—
Gripped with ready fore-paw!   On him a pouch there hung;
Wide it was and wondrous,   with cunning cordage strung,
And all y-wrought with artful thought,   of very dragon's skin,
By the craft of devil.   And me he'd thrust therein,
Me, a man unsinning,   and many another too—

77

This savage Prince-of-Evil.   But so he might not do,
When I myself in anger   stood there upright.
Too long it is to tell ye   how I did requite
This Scather of the people   for each deed of ill;
I did thy people honor,   my Lord, by strength and skill.
Away the Goblin scurried.   'T was but a little space
He still had joy of living.   But leaving there his trace,
His right paw in Heorot,   thence forlorn in fear,
Sick at heart, he fell into   the bottom of the mere.
 Hrothgar me rewarded   for that onset bold
Well with many a treasure,   yea, with plates of gold,
When had come the morning   and we sat at ale.
There was glee and singing.   Hrothgar hoar and hale,
Man of much adventure,   of far times told.
Whiles he touched the joy-wood,   the harp of man's delight,
He, the Brave-in-battle;   whiles would he recite
A lay of sooth and sadness;   whiles was he telling
Some legendary wonder,   he, the great-heart King.
Or whiles, again, that old Man,   the Warrior strook by time,
Began to mourn his lost youth,   the prowess of his prime.
His bosom welled within him,   when he, in years so grey,
Remembered so many things.   Thus we the live-long day
Partook there of desire,   until o'er sons of men
Another night was coming.   Soon thereafter then
Was faring forth in sorrow,   greedy to repay,
She, the Mother of Grendel.   Death had ta'en her son,—
Death and Geatmen's war-hate.   The eldritch Hag anon
Had her bairn avengéd,   killed a man with might:
From Aescher, old councillor,   the life took flight.
Nor could they, the Danefolk,   when the morning came,
Burn their perished comrade   with the brands of flame,
Nor lade upon the bale-fire   the dear Man there:

Beowulf

His corse beneath the mountain-streams   in devil-arms she bare.
O that was unto Hrothgar   the sorrowfullest stroke
Of all that long beset him,   this Chieftain of a folk.
   Then the grieving Sovran   begged me by thy life
To do a deed of earlship   amid the billows' strife,
To venture there my being   and win me renown.
He vowed to me a meed for that.   This Warden under mere,
I found, this Grim and Grisly,   this Wave-Thing widely known.
Hand to hand the twain of us   a while fought here.
With gore up-welled the waters;   off I carved the head
Of this Grendel's Mother   with a falchion dread,
In under-water hall of hers.   With life I got away,
Though sorely and barely—   as yet I was not fey.
Then did the Shield of jarlmen,   give, as erst he'd done,
To me full many a treasure,   Halfdane's Son.

XXXI

THE *Scop chants the conclusion of Beowulf's speech. (I suspect the Scribe should have made XXXI begin with line nine after Beowulf's speech.) Then the scop tells how Beowulf, according to courtly etiquette of those days, bestowed upon his King and the Queen the presents he had received at Heorot; and how King Hygelac rewarded Beowulf, his admirable nephew and glorious retainer, with a province in the Kingdom and a royal castle. He tells, too, something we*

79

had not guessed before—that Beowulf, like many another man of power in the world, was as a lad accounted slow and stupid. And a lad today, accounted slow and stupid, may comfort himself that perhaps he will grow up to be as brave and useful as Beowulf—for there are still many monsters infesting our halls and our happiness or prowling about the swamps by night, and strong men are needed for getting rid of them.

And now begins a new part of the story (which surely the Scribe should have made the beginning of the next fytte, XXXII). More than fifty years had passed since Beowulf, in his early twenties, had come back to Geatland in Scandinavia from slaying Grendel and his Mother in Daneland southward. He had now reigned fifty winters (the old Germanic tribes, like our Indians, reckoned years by 'winters'), when a Dragon, furious at treasure stolen from his hoard, began to make grievous trouble for the dwellers in the Kingdom.

THUS he kept, this Folk-King,   the customs of yore.
In naught was I the loser   of reward therefor,
Of meed for my prowess,—   nay, he gave me treasure,
He, the Kin of Halfdane,   to do with at my pleasure.
Now I will to bring them,   King of men, to thee,
To thee to proffer gladly.   From now what comes to me
Of good is all thy favor;   grievous is my lack
Of any closer kinsmen,   save thee, O Hygelac."
Then he bade to bear in   a banner with a boar,
And a towering war-helm,   and a byrnie hoar,
And a sword of splendor;   and spake with accents grave:
"To me this battle-garment   Hrothgar gave,
The wise son of Halfdane,   and added then his hest
That first I should relate thee   the tale of its bequest.
He quoth the Prince of Scyldings,   Heorogar, the King,
A long while had owned it,   this breast-garmenting;
But yet he would not give it   to son of his so lief,
Heoroward, the daring.   Enjoy it all, my chief."

Beowulf

I heard how as four horses,   alike in swiftness all,
Apple-fallow horses,   followed next in hall.
The gift of these and treasures   before his King he set;
So alway should a kinsman do   nor weave a wily net,
Nor plot with hidden cunning   a near companion's slaughter.
To Hygelac, the hardy,   the nephew was full leal,
And each was ever wistful   of the other's weal.
I heard how as the necklace   that she, the Prince's daughter,
Wealhtheow, had given him,   on Hygd he did bestow,
A curious wonder-jewel;   with palfreys three alsó,
Slender, bright-of-saddle.   After the bequest
The Lady wore the necklace   shining on her breast.

  So he bore him boldly,   bairn of Ecgtheow, he,
A man renowned for battles,   for deeds of bravery;
He lived in right and honor;   nor slew by foaming bowl
His comrades of the hearth-fire,   nor ruthless was of soul.
With utmost might of mankind   did he, the Battle-grim,
Guard the gift of strength that   God had granted him.
Scorned he'd been a long while;   the bairns of Geatish race
Good had not accounted him;   nor would the Weders' King
Make him on the mead-bench   worthy much of grace—
Slack the strong men weened him,   a sluggard aetheling:
But turn of fortune came to him,   as one with honors blest,
For every shame he'd suffered.   The King gave his behest,
He, the jarlmen's Bulwark,   then to fetch to hall
The heirloom of Hrethel,   with gold y-garnished all.
Never among the Geatmen   was aught in shape of blade
Ever a prize more goodly.   On Beowulf's lap he laid,
And gave him seven thousand,   a hall and high-seat.
Both possessed in common   hereditary land,
A home, an olden birth-right,   in country of the Geat,
Though th' Other's realm was broader,   since his a King's command.

Beowulf

It came to pass in after-days,   when Hygelac lay dead
After the battle-clashings,   and battle-swords had sped
Heardred, his offspring,   under the sheltering shield
(What time the hardy foeman,   the Scylfings, fierce in field,
Had sought him in the vanguard,   and laid him low with grame,
Nephew of Hereric),   that Beowulf became
Ruler of the broad realms.   Fifty winters told,
He reigned till now an agéd King,   a Folk-Ward old.
'Twas then that in the dark nights,   a Thing began to lord—
A Dragon on a hollow heath,   who watched there a hoard,
A steep stone-barrow.   A path thereunder lay,
By sons of men unguessed of.   There within did stray
Some nameless man or other,   who with hand did nim
From out the heathen Hoard, whilst   slept the Dragon grim,
A goblet, a golden one,   nor gave it back to him,
Albeit was thus defrauded   its Keeper thievishly. . . .
Then the folk in burgs around   found how wroth was he!

Beowulf

XXXII

THE *Scop is now well started on the story of the Dragon. He tells us some*
rious history: how it was a nameless slave, fleeing the wrath of his master (also
meless), who had entered by chance and discovered the Hoard; and how,
any, many, years before that luckless day some nobleman, the last of his race,
d hidden all that treasure there, and made a melancholy speech thereby. The
op goes on then to chant the wrath of the Dragon, who waited, like Grendel,
r the night, before making his attack on human kind.

BUT not of own accord there,   not of his own will,
Brake he the Serpent's Hoard there,   who did the Drake such ill;
But he, a slave of some one   of human fellowship,
Seeking forlorn for cover,   fled his master's whip,
And into the cave he entered,   a man by guilt oppressed.
Anon he gazed with terror,   he, the stranger guest;
Yet, even amid the horror,   he, the wretched wight,
Espied the jewelled goblet.   Was plain, besides, to sight
Many a treasure olden   in that house-of-earth,
Precious heirlooms golden   of kinsmen of high birth,
Which some jarl or other,   in the days of yore,
Taking thought, had hidden   there forevermore.
All his kin aforetime   death away had taken,
And he alone of warrior-host   lingering there forsaken,
A watcher, friends bewailing,   weened like theirs his doom,—
That soon he too must leave each   glad heirloom.
Ready to hand a barrow new   lay by ness and moor,
Hard-by the sea-waves,   secret and secure.
The Warden-of-Rings did thither   the jarl-treasure bear,
Of plated gold a goodly deal,   worth the hiding there.
Quoth he then in few words: "Earth, now hold,
Now that warriors can not,   the jarlmen's gold—

Beowulf

Lo, from thee did brave men   get it all of old.
Battle-death hath taken,   body-bale hath slain
Every sturdy fighter,   each folk-thane,
Of all who saw the joy in hall—   ne'er to see again.
None have I who'll wield the sword,   none who'll burnish fair
The golden-plated tankard,   the drink-stoup rare:
All the valiant noblemen   are gone . . . else . . . where.
From helmet hard, with gold dight,   the platings shall depart;
The burnishers are sleeping   who should prepare with art
The casques for every onset.   E'en so the army-coat,
That braved amid the battle   bite of steel on throat
Over the clashing bucklers,   shall crumble with its bearer;
Yea, the ringéd byrnie,   shall with its warrior-wearer
Fare afar no longer   on the hero's frame.
Never joy of harp now,   the glee-wood's game;
Never now the good hawk   swingeth through the hall;
Never now the swift horse   beateth court or stall;
Of my kith hath battle-death   sent . . . forth . . . all."
     Thus, with soul of sorrow,   alone he mourned the rest;
By day and night he wandered,   blitheless of breast,
Till waves of death o'erwhelmed him.   His Hoard of dead delight
That old Dusk-Scather,   who flieth in the night,
Enfolded in fire,   found all open there,—
That naked Poison-Dragon,   who, burning through the air,
Seeketh out the barrows.   Him the folk on fold
Dreadeth very sorely.   He needs must seek, I'm told,
For hoards within the earth and   guard the heathen gold,
A Worm of many winters—   no good thereby gets he!
So this Plague-of-people   for winters hundreds three,
This Drake so huge and mighty,   held within the ground
His own hoard-cavern,   until the man who found
Roused his wrath in bosom.   The golden tankard then

Beowulf

He bare unto his Master;   and begged for peace again
Of him, his angry Owner.   Thus plundered was the den,
The hoard of booty lessened.   The wretch received his boon.
His lord now first did look upon   the olden work of men;
And when the Worm awoke, there was   a new woe soon.
Along the stone he snuffed there,   this Stark-Heart dread,
And found the foeman's footprints,   who with secret tread
Had stepped there too forward   near his Dragon-head.
(Thus may a man not fey yet   survive, where'er he trod,
Woe and ways of exile   who owns the grace of God.)
Greedily the Hoard-Ward   sought along the ground
To find the man who gave his heart   asleep so sore a wound;
Hot and fierce, he circled   the barrow all around;
But in that barren moorland   not any man he found.
Yet war was in his marrow,   on battle-work his thought,—
Whiles darted into barrow,   the precious flagon sought.
Soon he found that some man   had searchéd out his gold,
His treasure-trove so lordly.   Though restive he and bold,
The Hoard-Ward bided   until the evening came;
Awrath the barrow's Keeper   would requite with flame
The dear drink-flagon. . . .   Now the day was fled,
To the joy of Dragon.   Blazing now he sped,
Folded in fire,   forth from the wall.
That was a beginning   horrible for all;
And folk within that Kingdom   soon thereafter kenned
In fate of their Ring-Giver   thereof the awful end.

Beowulf

XXXIII

THE *Scop chants how the Dragon burnt down with his fiery breath the home*
steads of men and even the castle of old King Beowulf; and how Beowulf, resolv
ing to do battle with this third Monster, alone as before, caused a shield of iron
to be made as protection against the Monster's spew of fire. The Scop then
recalls some of Beowulf's feats in days gone by: his fight with Grendel, of which
we have heard; his escape by swimming in the sea-raid of Hygelac into the land
of the Frisians (a raid which, as said, really took place in the sixth century, in
which King Hygelac lost his life); and how Beowulf had refused the offer of the
throne from the Queen-Widow, Hygd, preferring to act as unofficial adviser to
her son Heardred, till young King Heardred was slain by the Swedish King, Onela
for having sheltered Onela's rebellious and outlawed nephews.

THEN began the Stranger One   forth his gleeds to spew,
And burn the bright homesteads;   the glare ablazing flew,
Frightful to landsfolk.   Nothing living there
Would he leave, this loathly One,   Flier-in-the-air.
The warfare of the great Worm   wide about was clear,
The rancor of this Ravager,   afar and anear,—
How this fell Destroyer   the folk of Geatish kin
Hated and hounded.   He shot to Hoard within,
To his hidden King's-hall,   ere the morning came.
The dwellers in the land he'd   lapped about with flame,
With brand and with bale-fire.   He trusted in his mound,
His wall and his warfare.   His trust in vain he found.
    Then was unto Beowulf   the horror made known,
Speedily and soothly,   that the home his own,
The goodliest of dwellings,   the Geat's gift-throne,
In fiery surge had melted.   That to this good King
Was a grief in bosom,   the worst of sorrowing.
The Wise One he weenéd   that he the Wielder might

86

Beowulf

Bitterly have angered,   breaking olden right
Of the Lord eternal.   Welled his bosom sore
With thoughts of black foreboding,   as ne'er his wont before.
From beyond the water-land,   the Fire-Drake with gleeds
Now had laid in ashes   the fastness of the ledes,
The stronghold of Geatmen.   The Warrior-King for this,
The Sovran of the Weders, planned   how vengeance should be his.
He, the clansmen's Bulwark,   Lord of jarlmen, he,
Bade them work a wondrous shield,   all of iron firm—
For well he wist that linden,   wood of forest tree,
Could help him not against the flames   of that great Worm.
He needs must now be meeting,   this King of passing worth,
His end of days, the fleeting,   and his life on earth—
And the Dragon with him,   though long he held the Hoard.
Yet there he scorned, did Beowulf,   the Geats' Ring-Lord,
To follow the Far-Flier   with troops of spear and sword.
He dreaded not the contest,   despised the Dragon's war,
His vigor and his valor;   because so oft before,
He'd passed so many perils,   clashes in the van,
Hazarded so many straits,   since as victor-man,
He'd cleansed the hall of Hrothgar,   and at the grapple erst
Battling crushed the Grendel-kin—   that breed accurst.
   Nor least of fights was that fight   where Hygelac was slain,
When the King of Geatmen,   upon the Frisian plain,
The Lord-Friend of clansmen,   amid the battle-raid,
The offspring of Hrethel,   beaten down by blade,
Perished by the sword-drink.   Beowulf made shift,
'Scaping by a power his own,   his goodly swimming-gift.
He had upon his arms then,   though alone was he,
Thirty coats of armor,   as he plunged to sea.
O never the Hetwaras   boasted of that field
Who onward and before them   bore the linden-shield,

Beowulf

For few escaped the War-Wolf   to see again their home.
Then the son of Ecgtheow   o'erswam the tracts of foam,
A hapless man and lonely,   unto his folk again.
There Hygd to him did offer   the riches and the reign,
The rings and the King's seat.   Her bairn she did not trow
Fit to fend the Fatherland   from a foreign foe,
Now Hygelac had fallen.   Yet not for this could they,
The stricken, move the Aetheling   in purpose any way
To be the Lord of Heardred   and hold the kingdom's sway.
However, he upheld him   among the folk with lore,
With kindnesses of honor,   until, a lad no more,
Heardred wielded Weder-Geats.   Him o'er sea there sought
The outlaws, sons of Ohthere.   These had set at naught
The Helmet of the Scylfings,   the best of all sea-kings
Who ever there in Sweden   dealt the treasure-rings—
Onela, the high prince.   Heardred's end was that!
For sheltering the rebels   a mortal wound he gat
By swinges of the sword-blade.   And Bairn of Ongentheow
Departed for to seek his home,   at Heardred's overthrow,
Leaving unto Beowulf   the seat of ring-giving
And lordship over Geatmen—   that was a goodly King!

Beowulf

XXXIV

THE Scop, continuing his recollection of Beowulf's feats of old, chants how Beowulf, while still a young king, had, like Heardred, befriended Eadgils, son of Ohthere and rebel nephew of Onela, and avenged Heardred's death. And now the time had come for what was to be Beowulf's last feat of all. The slave who had found the cup was forced to show the way to the Dragon's cave down near the bleak ocean-cliffs. And Beowulf, with his eleven companions around him, sat down and talked, remembering old times. And he remembered particularly the fate of Hygelac's brother, Herebeald, accidentally shot by his other brother, Haethcyn, and the grief of the father, Hrethel, who had thus lost one son and who might not avenge his death on the slayer or even take blood-money from the slayer because the slayer was his son too. And as Beowulf thought of Hrethel's plight and grief, he imagined how sad it would be for an old king to see his son hanged for murder. Beowulf's speech is well in accord in mood with his forebodings of his own impending fate; but does it not seem odd he should have been speaking at such length on matters so far from the business awaiting him? You and I feel that the Scop is forgetting the Dragon, and making Beowulf forget the Dragon; and because we haven't forgotten him, we chide the Scop or don't listen very attentively.

IN AFTER-DAYS did Beowulf   bethink him to requite
The downfall of Heardred;   and that wretched Wight,
Eadgils, he befriended;   Ohthere's son did he
Aid with a folk-band   across the broad sea,
With warriors and weapons;   and Eadgils then was bold
To slay the King in payment   for paths of exile cold.
So the son of Ecgtheow   had 'scapéd every harm
Of strife and stern encounter,   by works of sturdy arm,
Until the day 't was his at last   to battle with the Worm.
    He went with his eleven,   wroth exceedingly,
He, the King of Geatmen,   the Fire-Drake to see.

Beowulf

He 'd heard for why had risen   this feud, this deadly hap;
The treasure-cup its finder's hand   had given into his lap;
And he whose luckless finding   that warfare all began
Was, amid that company,   the thirteenth man.
A captive, a craven,   't was his in cringing sorrow
Thence to lead the way along   unto the moor and barrow;
Against his will he footed   until the mound he found,
The one and only earth-hall,   the cavern under ground,
Near the ocean billows,   near the surges' sound.
Within 't was full of jewels,   of wire-work in gold;
And the frightful Watcher   did the treasure hold,
Ready for the battle,   the Old One in his lair—
'T was no easy bargain   for men to enter there!

Upon the ness he sat him,   the King in battles bred;
Gold-Friend of Geatmen,   while farewell he said
To all his hearth-fellows.   His thoughts were sad and grim,
Wavering and deathward;   and all too nigh to him
Wyrd was there awaiting   to greet that agéd Heart,
Aye, to seek his soul's hoard,   to sunder apart
The life from the body.   Not long it was before
The spirit of the Aetheling   was wound in flesh no more.

Beowulf made his speech then,   son of Ecgtheow, he:
"From many a battle onset   in youth I 'scapéd free,
From many a while of warfare—   I mind me of them all.
I was seven winters,   when from father's hall
That Prince-of-people took me,   that Giver-of-the-Ring.
He held me, he had me,   Hrethel, he, the King;
Fee and food he gave me,   of kinship mindful, he;
Never was I loathlier   to him in grace and gree,
While a bairn in burg I lived,   than his sons, the three,
Herebeald and Haethcyn,   or my Hygelac.

Beowulf

[For Herebeald, the eldest,   by unmeet attack,
By the deed of Kinsman,   was strewn the death-bed,
When Haethcyn with arrow,   from horn-bow sped,
Smote his own Herebeald,   his Liege-Lord, dead;
He missed of his mark there,   and shot his Kinsman's heart,
A brother the other,   with a bloody dart.
That was a fight all fee-less,   of sin a fearful thing,
A horror unto Hrethel,   and yet the Aetheling,
Forever unavengéd,   must from life depart.
It were a sight too awful   for agéd man to bide,
To see his boy, his young boy,   upon the gallows ride.
Then his lay he moaneth,   his sorrow-song he speaks,
When his son is hanging,   a joy for ravens' beaks;
And he may help him no wise,   this old man forlorn.
And he is reminded,   each and every morn,
Of his bairn gone elsewhere.   Nor doth the father care
To see within his burg-hall   now another heir,
Since the one in death-pangs   had suffered evil so.
Upon his son's own bower,   he looketh, worn with woe—
The wine-hall a waste now,   where the winds sweep,
Bereft now of revel.   The rider is asleep,
The warrior in his under-grave;   there is with harp no glee,
And in the courts no wassail,   as there used to be.]

Beowulf

XXXV

(I THINK *the Scribe should have begun this division with the second para*
graph. At least that is where I will begin here in my introduction and summary.

After the unhappy King Hrethel's death—so continued Beowulf's reminis
cences—war broke out again between the Geats and the Swedes (whose territory
was not exactly the Sweden of today, but a smaller region just north of the trib
of the Geats). Here Haethcyn fell. Here the Swedish King, Ongentheou
fell too, slain by Eofor. Here too Beowulf performed brave deeds, as he di
likewise later on the raid into Frisia, when Beowulf slew a certain Daeghrefr
presumably the slayer of Hygelac. Beowulf, in this long speech of his, now a
last bethought him of the Dragon. (I wonder what the Dragon had been doin
meanwhile—had he begun to tremble at a foeman with such a warlike record?
And the Scop chants how Beowulf stood up and roared his challenge into th
cavern, and how, apparently somewhat inside the entrance, the fight began; an
how Beowulf's sword crumpled under the blow he wielded, and how Beowulf i
deadly peril was forced to back out, and how his chosen band of braves miserabl
fled into the woods, all except one.

[TO BED then he goeth;   chanteth a sorrow-song,
   The lone one for the lost one.   Seemeth all too wide
His fields and his homestead. . . .   So it did betide
The Helmet of the Weders;   his welling heart must long
Ever after Herebeald,   but yet the bloody wrong
He might not venge on Haethcyn,   by whom the brother died.
Nor even might he hound him,   the warrior he begot,
By loathly deed of hatred,   albeit he loved him not.
And so then for the sorrow   he suffered from these blows,
The mirth of men he gave up   and God's light chose.
He left unto his offspring   (as doth a man of pelf)
His land and his folk-burgs,   when death had ta'en himself.
   Then rose there crime and conteck   the Swedes and Geats between

Beowulf

Over the wide water,—   a conflict close and keen,
A war-hate of the hardy,   after Hrethel died,
And the sons of Ongentheow   were forward in their pride,
And would not hold the peace-pact   with folk beyond the sea.
But raided oft round Hreosnabeorh   in forays fierce and free.
That strife my friends and kinsmen   repaid, as all men know,
That unholy warring;   albeit another, though,
Bought with life the victory,   a price not low—
To Haethcyn, Lord of Geatmen,   was that fighting fell.
But upon the morrow,   as I heard tell,
One brother the other   avenged right well
With sword upon the murderer,   when Eofor met the King,
And war-helm of Ongentheow   was split in plate and ring,
And battle-wan he dropped adown,   this old Scylfing.
O Eofor's hand that smote him   had not forgot, I trow,
The former feuds aplenty,   nor withheld the blow!]

My master I repaid in war   with my sword so bright,
For treasures he had given me,   as fully as I might.
With land had he endowed me,   with stead and joy of home;
He had no need to seek him   from Danes across the foam,
From Gifths or realm of Sweden,   a worser warrior-wight,
And buy the same with wages.   Always I the man
To fight before the foremost,   alone before the van;
And so forever shall I fight   long as this sword shall last
That hath so often served me   in years now past,
Ere since before the warriors   'twas mine to slay with hand
Daeghrefn, Champion   of the Frankish band.
The spoils of slaughtered Hygelac   it was not his to bring,
Not his, those deckings of the breast,   unto the Frisian King;
But in the fight he crumpled, he,   banner-bearer too,
This Aetheling of prowess;   nor was't the sword that slew,

Beowulf

But my battling arm-grip   his bone-house broke,
And stopped his heart's surgings.   And now by falchion's stroke
By hand and by hard blade,   I 'll battle for the Hoard."
    Beowulf made his speech then;   spake a vaunting word,
Even for the last time: "Lo, I dared my fill
Of battles in my youth, I.   Now this day I will,
The folk's old Warden,   dare another still,
And do a deed of glory,   if this Pest-of-all
Forth will come to seek me   from his earth-hall."
    Then each man he greeted,   the helmet-bearers grim,
Even for the final time,   his fellows dear to him:
"No sword would I bear me,   no weapon to this Snake,
If I only wist how   to get upon the Drake
The boasted grip of arm that I   once on Grendel got.
But yonder I do fear me   battle-fire hot,
Reek of breath and poison.   And so I have on me
Shield-board and byrnie.   No foot-breadth I 'll flee
From the barrow's Keeper.   Us twain it shall befall,
Even as Wyrd allotteth,   fighting at the wall—
Wyrd who is the master   ever of us all.
My mood is bold and I forbear   my boast against this Flyer.
Bide ye by the barrow,   in your war-attire,
Ye heroes in your harness,   awaiting which of twain
Shall better bear the onset   and the battle-pain.
This quest is not for you now,   but mine alone the meed
To match a might with Monster   and do a jarlman's deed.
I 'll win this gold with prowess,   or war shall take me hence—
The death-bale take the fighting man,   your dear Prince."
    Upstood beside his buckler   this Man-at-arms so stark,
Hardy under helmet.   He bore his battle-sark
Down beneath the stone-cliff.   He trusted at the test
The strength of one man only—   not that a craven's quest!

Beowulf

Then he who'd passed in hardihood   unscathed so many blows,
So many battle-rushes   where clashed afoot the foes,
Espied by the wall there   a stone-arch stout,
Whence a stream was breaking   from the barrow out.
The billows of that burn there   were hot with fierce fire;
Nor that under-passage,   to the Hoard nigher,
Might he any while endure,   for the Dragon's flare.
From his breast he let then   a word forth fare,
He, the Prince of Weder-Geats,   swelling in his ire.
The Stark-Heart storméd.   His battle-clear tone
Went aringing inward   under the hoar stone.
Dragon-hate was rouséd;   the Hoard-Ward knew
'T was indeed the voice of man.   Now between the two
Was no time for peace-pact!
                  First from out the gloom
Burst the breath of Monster,   hot battle-fume.
The hollow earth resounded.   Against the grisly Guest
Beowulf in barrow   swung his shield to chest;
Then Ring-Bow in heart was   ready for the test.
But the goodly War-King   had drawn his sword for blow,
An old-time heirloom,   with edge not slow.
Each with thoughts of murder felt   terror of his foe.
Stern of mood, the Chieftain stood   against his buckler high.
The Worm now arched its back amain.   The Mailed One waited nigh.
With body bowed it burned and glode,   hastening to its fate;
But shield did fend in life and limb   the King so good and great
A briefer while than wish of him   did thereby await:
For there 't was his to struggle   the first time and day
In such a wise as Wyrd denies   victory in the fray.
He had his hand uplifted,   he, the Geatish Lord;
Hard smote the grisly Foeman   with the ancient sword;
But, lo, its edge did crumble,   brown upon the bone,

And bit there too slackly   for need of Hero lone,
In the press of sore distress.   The barrow's Keeper then
After that battle-swingeing   was mad of mood again;
He scattered fires of slaughter;   and wide sprang the flame.
The Gold-Friend of Geatmen   bragged no victory-fame.
His war-bill weakened,   naked in the feud,
As it ever ought not,   an iron passing good.
That was no easy faring   back o'er cavern's ground
For the Kin of Ecgtheow,   the far-renowned.
'T was his against his will now   to make his home elsewhere,
To leave the life that 's loaned us,   as every man must fare.
Anon the infuriate Foemen   again together drew;
Heartened himself the Hoard-Ward,   and belched his breath anew;
And he who once had wielded   over a folk as Sire
Was laboring now in sore straits,   folded round with fire.
Nor stood about him staunchly   his own fighting crew,
The bairns of the aethelings;   but to the woods they flew,
And there they saved their bodies.   On one of them this wrought
Cark and care of spirit: there is never aught
Can alter loyal kinship   for man of noble thought.

Beowulf

XXXVI

THE *Scop chants of Wiglaf, the one faithful brave retainer, a young kinsman* Beowulf. *Wiglaf had a sword, inherited from his father, as many swords in* ose *days were handed down from father to son; his father had taken it in battle* om *Eanmund, one of those two Swedish outlaw-princes; and with this good* ord *in hand he upbraided the coward companions.   (But how could Beowulf,* experienced *and wise, have picked out for special honor young warriors who so* eadfully *betrayed his confidence?   Perhaps Beowulf, so generous and brave* mself, *always had a childlike faith in the generosity and bravery of his retainers.* any *great men, too, are so intent on their great works that they lack practical* rewdness *in judging the weaknesses of their fellowmen—perhaps that was the* se *with Beowulf.)   Wiglaf then rushed up to aid Beowulf and the twain to-* ther *fought the Dragon; but Beowulf's sword, Naegling, was shivered and the* ragon *got its fangs into Beowulf's neck.   (What the Scop says about the sword* puzzling. *He says Beowulf's strength was so great that every sword went to* eces *when he wielded it; yet Beowulf had a sword so dear to him that it bore a* ecial *name, and besides had not Beowulf himself boasted before of his victor-* ows *with the sword?   Perhaps the Scop has made use of two different traditions* out *Beowulf,—a tradition of Beowulf brave in battle, bearing like other great* arriors *a good sword, and another tradition, probably the more wide-spread and* d, *of Beowulf as the Strong Man who needed no weapon.   Or perhaps, after all,* was *only* sometimes *that Beowulf found that a sword shivered in his mighty* m.)

HIGHT was that one Wiglaf,   the son of Weohstan,
    And Lord of the Scylfings,   belovéd Shield-man,
Aelfhere's kinsman.   His Liege-Lord he saw
Under his casque of battle   front that flaming maw.
Then he recalled the giftings   from him his Lord and Head,—
The lands of the Waegmundings,   the rich homestead,
And each of all the folk-rights   his father used to wield.

Beowulf

No longer might he hold back;   his fingers clasped the shield,
The wood of yellow linden;   his olden sword he drew.
   This sword was Eanmund's relic,   as all men knew,
Whom in the fray by falchion-edge   Weohstan slew—
Eanmund, son of Ohthere,   the exile forlorn.
And Weohstan to Eanmund's Kin,   Onela, had borne
The brown-bright helmet,   the byrnie of the rings,
The old sword of ettins,—   Eanmund's battle-things,
The war-gear furbished   of a brother's son;
But these did Onela return   to Weohstan anon,
Nor spake of feud for slaughter   Weohstan had done.
These trappings Weohstan retained   for many years his own,
The bill and the byrnie,   until his boy had grown
Strong for deeds of jarlman   like his father's feats.
He gave them to Wiglaf,   now among the Geats,
War-weeds unnumbered,   as he fared from life,
Old upon his forth-way.

               And now in battle-strife
'Twas Wiglaf's for the first time   to serve beside his Lord.
Nor did his spirit soften,   nor did his father's sword
Weaken in the war-fare—   as soon he found, the Drake,
When once they'd met together!   Wiglaf he spake;
Said to comrades sagely,   as sorrow sore he dreed:
"The time I well remember,   as we took the mead,
How we vowed in beer-hall   to him who gave us rings,
Vowed unto our Overlord,   that we, his aethelings,
Would requite for war-gear,   for hard sword and helm,
If need like this should haply   ever overwhelm.
For this it was he chose us,   us for this his quest,
Of his own will, and deemed us   worth the glorious test.
And gave to me these treasures,   because he counted us
Good spear-wielders,   helmets valorous,

Beowulf

Albeit our Lord was minded,   as Fender of his folk,
Himself alone to compass   for us the victor-stroke,
Since he of men hath compassed   most of glory-fray,
Most of deeds of daring.   Now is come the day
Our Master needs the prowess   of war-men good.
Let us hasten to him,   to help his hardihood,
Whilst the heat is round him,   the grim horror-fire.
Of me, at least, God wotteth   it is my dear desire
That flame embrace this body mine   with his who gave me gold.
Methinketh it unseemly   our bucklers home to bring
Before we fell the foe and   save the Weders' King.
Well I wot it suits not   with all his deeds of old
That he, alone of Geatland's   tried men and bold,
Should suffer this sorrow   and sink in battle down.
Sword, helm, byrnie, shield,   between us shall be one."
   Then strode he through the slaughter-reek   with casque upon his head,
To be the standby of his Lord.   A few words he said:
"Beowulf, belovéd,   hold here, hold,
Even as in young days   sworest thou of old
Ne'er to let thy glory fall,   so long as life should be.
'T is thine, O steadfast Aetheling,   famed in bravery,
To guard thee now with all thy prow.   I will succor thee."
   At the words the Worm came   a second time in ire,
Shining in the surging flame,   Stranger fierce and dire,
To seek his Foes, the loathéd men.   Was burnt in waves of fire
His buckler to the very boss.   Nor yet his byrnie might
Serve to shelter Wiglaf,   the young Spear-Wight.
So dodged the Youth right speedily   his Kinsman's shield behind,
Now his own was all consumed   by the fury-wind.
Then again the War-King   his glory called to mind,
And smote he then by main-strength   with his battle-glaive,
That, under impulse of his hate,   to the head it drave.

But Naegling was shivered: failed him in the fray,
This the sword of Beowulf,   etched and old and gray.
To him it was not given   that any edge of brand
Him could help at battle;   so strong his arm and hand,
As I have heard the story,   that every blade so'er
He overtaxed in swinging it,   when he to battle bare
A weapon wondrous hardy.   'T would stead him not a whit.
    Then was the People-Scather,   a third time too,
This bold Fire-Dragon,   mindful to do;
He rushed upon the Hero,   where his chance was fit,
Hot and battle-ugly.   All the neck he bit
With his bitter fang-teeth.   To death the Geat was hurt,
Bloodied o'er with his own gore,   in welling wave and spurt.

XXXVII

THE Scop chants how Wiglaf succeeded in piercing the Dragon in the b
(where the hide was softer and where probably there were no protecting scale
and how the dying Beowulf then cut him down the middle with his war-kn
And so an end to the Dragon. But Beowulf sat down a little before the cave
entrance, while Wiglaf ministered to him. Then he spoke, reconciled to dec
because he felt he had lived the good life, as defender of his homeland, as a n
of his word, and as one who had not murdered his kinsmen (as so many ch
and kings used to do). And he bade Wiglaf go and fetch forth some of
treasure.

THEN at the need of Beowulf,   as I heard tell,
The Jarlman upstanding   proved his prowess well,
His craft and his keenness,   as his indeed by birth.
He made not for the Monster's head;   but in his will and worth,
His hand was all but burnt away,   the while he helped his Kin,

Beowulf

As pierce he did the flamy Drake   from under, up and in,—
This Hero in his harness.   Deep the sword it ran,
Gleaming and gold-dight.   And the fire began
To slacken thereafter.   The King himself once more
Girt his wits together.   His war-knife he drew,
Biting and battle-sharp,   which on his sark he wore.
The Weder down the middle then   slit the Worm in two.
So they felled the Dragon,   the fiery head and wings.
The dauntless twain the Pest had slain,   Kinsman-Aethelings.
Each warrior it behooveth   like Wiglaf to be,
Each thane at need of liege-lord.
                                    But for the King was this
The last of victor-hours   by any deed of his,
The last of work in world here.   The wound he had to dree
From the Snake of under-earth   began to burn and swell;
And soon he found a poison   balefully did well
Deep in breast within him.   Walked the King along,
Till by the wall he sate him,   thinking, on the mould;
He looked upon the giants' works,—   the earth-house old
With arches there-under   on posts stone-strong.
Then with hands his Wiglaf,   retainer without peer,
Laved him with water,   his Overlord dear,
Laved the bleeding Hero,   battle-worn and drear,
And loosened him his helmet.
                                    Beowulf replied,
Spake, in spite of deadly wound   pitifully wide;
Well he weened his time was come,   his earth-joys passed,
His tale of days all taken,   and death anearing fast:
"Now would I give over,   now unto my son,
To offspring, my war-weeds,   if me were granted one—
An heir from my body,   to wear them when I died.
I have ruled this people   fifty winters' tide;

Beowulf

Nor is there any folk-king of all who dwell around
That durst me touch with sword of his, or me with terrors hound.
I bided in my homeland my appointed while;
Well mine own I warded; nor practiced feud and wile;
Nor sware, I guess, not many broken oaths of guile.
Of all of this my joy I have, though ill of wounds within,
Since me the God of men may not charge with murdered kin,
When life my body leaveth. . . . Go, now, quick,
To look upon the Hoard there under the hoar stone,
Wiglaf, belovéd, . . . now the Worm is prone,
And sleepeth, reft of treasure-trove, from the sword so sick.
Wiglaf, hasten now, that I may once behold
These riches of the foretime, these master-stores of gold. . . .
Yea, that once with gladness I may look upon
The bright and cunning jewels. For softlier anon,
After that golden seeing, I'll leave behind, I know,
My life and the lordship I held from long ago."

Beowulf

XXXVIII

THE *Scop chants how Wiglaf, at the dying Beowulf's bidding, went and* tched *all the treasure he could carry and laid it before Beowulf; and how Beo-* ulf, *generously thinking of his people to the last, thanked God that he had won* em *such golden gifts; and how, thinking too of his fame in aftertimes, he gave* structions *for a memorial mound on the promontory; and how, in gratitude* *his loyal young Kinsman, he gave Wiglaf his collar and war-gear, and passed* *his reward among those who had lived righteously on earth. (Here are two* uestions *for us: was Beowulf a Christian? and did Wiglaf become King of the* eats?)

THEN the son of Weohstan,   as I heard tell,
   Swiftly stirred to wish and word   of him whose wound was fell,
Of him the battle-sick Man;   and under barrow's roof
Took himself and ring-mesh,   his woven sark of proof.
And then that dauntless Thane-man   saw with victor-pride,
On passing where his Chieftain sate,   store of gems inside:
Saw the gold glisten   on the ground then,
Wonders on the wall there,   and the Dragon's den,
Flier old by twilight,   of standing jars a sight,
Vessels of the men of yore,   with none to burnish bright,
Bereft of their adornments.   Many a helmet old
There was lying rusty,   and arm-rings of gold,
Artfully twisted.   (Riches so rare,
Such booty in a barrow,   may easily ensnare
Any one of mankind,   hide it whosoe'er.)
And also saw he hanging   over Hoard on high
A banner all golden,   wefted cunningly,
Of handiwork a wonder.   And from it streamed a light,
Whereby the cavern's bottom   well perceive he might,
And well o'er-count the prizes.   But saw not there within

Any sign of Serpent— sword had taken him
  Then, as I heard the story, did one Man alone
Reave the Hoard from olden mound, the giants' work of stone;
With beakers and with platters, as his choice would seek,
He laded his bosom. He took the banner eke,
Brightest of beacons. The old King's bill—
O its edge was iron!— a while ago did kill
Him who had defended so long the treasure-found,
And spread o' midnights terror-flames, billowing fiercely round,
Hot before the Hoard there, until he died of wound.
Hastened now the Herald, eager to go back,
Spurred by splendor-booty. Him a doubt did rack
Whether he, the high-souled, would meet alive once more
The Sovran of the Weders, weakened now so sore,
There upon the moor-stead where him he'd left before.
  Then Wiglaf with the treasures found his King and Friend,
His glorious Chief, ableeding, near his life's end.
Again he plashed with water; until the point of word
Pierced athrough the breast-hoard of Beowulf, the old,
And spake he in his grieving, with gaze upon the gold:
"For this splendor-booty be thanks unto the Lord,
Unto the King-of-Glory, for what I here behold,
To God, the everlasting, in that 't is mine to give
Such gifts unto my people, while an hour I live.
Now have I bartered for the hoard of gold
The end of this my old life. Look ye well, my fere,
To my people's needs now. I'm no longer here.
Bid the battle-bold men build a mound to me,
Shining, after death-pyre, on foreland by the sea;
Out upon Whale's Ness, it shall lift on high,
Reminder to my people of the man was I,
That ever thereafter sailor-folk will hail

Beowulf

'Beowulf's Barrow'   when home from far they sail,
O'er the misty ocean,   past the Ness-of-Whale."
   From his neck he doffed then,   he, the Sturdy-Souled,
And gave to his Retainer,   a collar of gold;
Gave the young Spearman   his helmet gold-bedight,
His ring and his byrnie;   bade him use them right:
"Thou art only remnant   of our common line,
The Kin of the Waegmundings,   Wiglaf mine.
Wyrd has swept before ye   all my stock and stem,
The jarlmen in their glory.   I must after them."
The last of words was that for which   that agéd Heart had breath,
Ere he chose the bale-fire,   the hot waves of death.
And so from breast of Beowulf   the soul took flight
To seek the just award of souls   soothfast in the right.

XXXIX

THE *Scop chants how the Dragon was surely dead too; and how the cowardly deserters emerged shame-faced from the woods, and how Wiglaf upbraided them as ingrates and poltroons. (The simple men of those days thought there was no crime more shameful than disloyalty; and some wise philosophers of today have told me those simple men were right.)*

THEN it went O sorely   with the young Friend,
   When he saw his dearest   at his life's end,
Faring so pitiful—   his King upon the ground.
But lay the Slayer likewise,   wasted with a wound,

Beowulf

Of his life bereavéd,   Earth-Drake vile—
No longer crook-bow worm could lord   o'er the treasure-pile,
Since the edge of iron,   forged by hammer's play,
Blade so hard and battle-scarred,   had ta'en him far away.
Thus the Wide-Flier,   from his wound so still,
Sprawled upon the mould there,   nigh his hoard-hill.
Nevermore o' midnights   would he disport in air,
Or, proud of his prizes,   show his shadow there.
But he to earth had fallen,   by the work of hands
Of a Battle-Leader.   Forsooth, in all the lands
But few, however hardy   and dauntless of deed,
Have thriven when they bravéd   the breath of Poison-Breed,
Or when they laid their hands on   a drake's ring-hall,
If once they found the Warden   watching by the wall,
Crouching at the barrow—   few, as I recall.
This deal of lordly goods was bought   by Beowulf's own death;
And each from out this fleeting life   yielded up his breath.
    Ere long the battle-laggards,   the troth-breaking men,
The woodland abandoned,   together the ten,
That durst not there awhile ago   put their spears in play
For Beowulf, their Liege-Lord,   in his mickle needs;
But each one bore his buckler   and his battle-weeds,
Shambling and shame-faced,   to where the Old One lay.
And they looked on Wiglaf.   He o'erwearied kneeled
At his Master's shoulder,   he, so brave with shield;
Would waken him with water.   But help was none thereby,
And the Youth he might not,   though yearned he so to try,
Hold on earth the life of him   whom God had willed should die.
God, the mighty Deemster,   wielded his will
Then o'er deeds of human kind   as he doeth still.
There was in the young Thane   an answer grim withal,
Nor hard of understanding,   to those cowards all.

Beowulf

Wiglaf made a speech then,   son of Weohstan,
Gazing broken-hearted   at each hated man:
"Lo, whoso will speak sooth,   can say one thing:
That, when he gave ye good gear,   he, your Lord and King,
Gave the battle-harness   ye are standing in,
He threw away those war-weeds,   unto shame and sin,
When the fight befell him—   and oft enough withal
Bestowed he at the ale-bench   on sitters in the hall,
This King unto his clansmen,   helm and byrnie-gear,
The finest he could find for ye,   from afar or near.
In sooth had he, your Folk-King,   little cause to vaunt
Of comrades in this conquest!   But God was kind to grant,
The Wielder over victories,   that with knife, alone,
When he had need of valor,   he laid the Monster prone.
Little could I offer   of aid at the fight,
Yet I helped my Kinsman   beyond my might.
When I struck the deadly   Foeman with my sword,
Thereby was he the weaker   and the slower poured
The fire from the wits of him.   Of helpers, small the sum
That thronged around the Chieftain   when his hour had come.
How shall fail forever   for your Kin abhorred
The getting of the gold-rings,   the gifting of the sword,
All the mirth of land of birth.   Every man shall roam,
Beggared of his freehold,   from his burg and home,
When aethelings from far away   shall hear your deed of blame,
This your flight, ye cowards.   For one of jarlman's name,
Death itself is better   than a life of shame."

Beowulf

XL

THE *Scop chants how Wiglaf sent a Herald (who must have been one of the ten coward-companions) to report the issue of the fight to the little army of Beowulf which was waiting, perhaps a few miles away. (One remembers Beowulf had refused to let them come with him, for he had said he wished to face the danger alone with only eleven men.) The Herald told them all. He had little joy over the dead Monster, for thinking of the wars that would come to the Geats, when their old enemies, the Frisians and the Swedes, should hear about him, the Folk Defender, whom the Dragon had slain. And the Herald retold to the warriors (who surely must have known as much about it as he!) the story of the old wars with these tribes. (The Scop has touched on these stories a good many times, when we grew confused or did not listen, and when we wished he would keep to the story of Beowulf at Heorot or Beowulf at the Dragon's Lair. But those for whom the Scop composed and recited the poem were doubtless stirred by these traditions of bygone battles of their kindred and felt that they were not out of harmony in spirit and action with Beowulf's own adventures.)*

THEN Wiglaf bade a Herald   the war-work to declare
    Yonder at the fastness   o'er the sea-cliff there,
Where the band of shieldmen   had sat in brooding pain
All the long morning,   between doubts twain:
The end of their belovéd, or . . .   his coming-home again.
Of these new tidings   the Rider to the ness
Was silent touching little;   nay, in soothfastness
He told out the story   in ears of all the band:
"Now is he, Joy-Giver   of the Weder-land,
The Sovran of the Geatmen,   on the couch-of-death,—
He woneth on the slaughter-bed,   from Dragon's tooth and breath.
Is lying there beside him   the Queller of the Good,
Sick with thrusts of dagger;   for with the sword he could
Work no wound soever,   upon the Monster's hide.

Beowulf

Wiglaf is sitting,   Beowulf beside,
Weohstan's youngling,   the quick beside the dead.
Holdeth he with heart's woe   a watch at his head,
O'er loved Lord and loathed Drake.
                                    Now our folk may wait
Anew a while of warfare   when our Prince's fate
Unto Franks and Frisians   shall be widely told.
Started was this quarrel   grievously of old,
When Hygelac to Frisian land   afaring came with fleet.
And him the Hetwaras   did in battle beat,
And valiantly achievéd   by their over-might
That he, the byrnie-breasted,   bowed and fell in fight—
To give unto his chivalry   no more the treasures bright.
And ever thereafter   could our Geatish clan
Count on little kindness from   the Merovingian.
    Nor do I wait from Swedefolk   aught but fray and feud—
For widely couth the story is   how Ongentheow, the good,
Slaughtered Haethcyn, Hrethel's son,   off at Ravenswood.

[In wanton over-weening,   in earlier times before,
We Geatish folk had ravaged   the Scylfings great in war;
Anon Ohthere's father,   the ancient Ongentheow,
Old and full of fury,   gave a counter-blow,
Killed the Viking Haethcyn,   and freed his captive wife,—
The venerable lady,   berobbed of gold in strife,
She who'd born him Onela   and Ohthere of yore,—
And followed then the foemen,   until, forlorn and sore,
They hid themselves in Ravensholt,   their Leader being dead.
Ongentheow beset then,   with a host outspread,
This remnant of the carnage   with wounds o'erweariéd.
The live-long night he menaced   with woe the wretched herd:
With sword-edge in the morning   he'd mow them, was his word,

109

Or hang them on the gallows-tree,   a sport for every bird.
But comfort to the downcast   came with dawn of day,
When heard they horn of Hygelac   and trumpet boom away,
As fared he on the track of them   with his war-array.]

XLI

The Scop chants the rest of the Herald's speech about the old wars; and he strikes some melancholy music on his harp, and goes on to tell how the warsmen in tears went to look upon their dead Leader and saw too the dead Beast of Evil and the Treasure.

[THE bloody swath of Swedes and Geats   the fighters' slaughter-storr
Was seen afar, how either folk   waked alike the harm.
So he went, did Ongentheow,   with his arméd men,
This Agéd, sorely sorrowful,   to seek his fastness then;
Yes, Ongentheow turned round to go   up to his burg again.
He'd learned about the hardihood   of Geatman Hygelac,
The war-craft of the Proud One;   he dared no counter-strife,
He knew not his the ablesse   these sea-men to attack,
Or 'gainst these sailor-foes to fend   hoard and bairns and wife.
And so unto his earth-wall   the Old One bent him back,—
The Geatfolk chased the Swedefolk   and flags of Hygelac
O'er their fended refuge   forward forged along,

Beowulf

After his Victor-Hrethlings   did to the ramparts throng.
   But in that battle Ongentheow,   the King with locks of gray,
By the edges of the swords   was brought at last to bay;
And forced to dree the sole doom   that Eofor's wrath did will:
Wulf, the son of Wonred,   had strook the King with bill,
Even so that under blow   sprang from veins the blood,
Out beneath his hair then.   But fearlessly he stood,
And paid anon with better one   for the slaughter-wound,
As he, the King, the old Scylfíng,   had turned on him around.
And the swift Wonreding   no counter-buffet gave
Before the Jarl, that ancient carl,   his head and helmet clave.
So Wulf, the son of Wonred,   must bow, with gore bewet;
He tottered to the greensward,   but fey was he not yet;
And well he waxed thereafter,   albeit the wound was grave.
'T was then the hardy Eofor,   thane of Hygelac,
E'en where Wulf, his brother, lay,   over shield did hack
The giant helm of Ongentheow,   with his broad glaive,
His old sword of ettins.   The King he bowed in strife;
The Shepherd of his people   was smitten to the life.
And then were there many   the brother's wounds to bind,
And him to lift with speedy shift,   when 't was theirs to find
Themselves the masters of the field.   And in the meanwhile now
One warrior reaved the other—   Eofor Ongentheow.
He took the iron byrnie,   helm and hilted sword,
And bare the Hoar One's harness   to Hygelac, his Lord.
He received the war-spoils,   and fairly pledged the Youth
A boon before the people—   and kept his pledge in sooth.
For the Lord of Geatmen,   son of Hrethel's name,
Rewarded for that onset,   when as home he came,
Eofor and Wulf both,   with treasure manifold;
To each of them he yielded,   in measure of gold,
Of land and interlinkéd rings   a hundred thousand told.

Beowulf

And no man in this Middle-Yard   had cause that boon to blame,
Seeing the two with strokes of swords   had wrought such deeds of fame.
And as a pledge of favor,   to Eofor for bride
He gave his only daughter,   of his home the pride.]

This is the feud and hating,   the deadly strife of men,
Wherewith, as I'm awaiting,   the Swedes will seek us then,
They, the battling Scylfings,   for their heroes slain,
As they shall learn the loss of   him our Overlord,
Him who once had guarded   our Kingdom and the hoard,
And furthered the folk-weal,   and done a jarlman's deed.
    Now is best that thither   we hasten with speed
To look upon our people's Sire,   and Beowulf to bring
Onward to the funeral pyre,   who gave us ring by ring.
Nor shall a portion only   melt with the man so bold,
But there is a hoard of treasures,   and there is countless gold,
Purchased forsooth at a grim price,—   circlet and sword and pelf,
Bought us now at the latest   with life of the King himself.
These shall the fire devour,   these shall the flame enfold;
Never a jarl shall bear him   a token dear of the King,
No beautiful girl shall wear gem   on neck in a noble ring;
But each, of the gold bereavéd,   each in a mood of pain,
Shall wander the lands of strangers,   over and over again,
Now that the Army-Leader   hath lowered his laughter here,
His mirth and the joy of his revel.   For this shall many a spear,
Iron-cold in the morning,   be lifted up in the arm,
Clasped in the clansman's fingers;   and never the harper's charm
Shall waken these of our warriors.   Nay, but the raven wan,
Fluttering over the fallen,   shall utter his croak anon,
Telling unto the eagle   how he at his feasting sped,
The while with the wolf together   he tore away on the dead."
    Thus it was the Warsman   the loathly tidings said;

Beowulf

Little was he lying   in words or doom ahead.
Together rose the band then,   with tears of sorrow-stress,
Blitheless they betook them   under Eagles' Ness,
To gaze upon the wonder.   They found o'er sandy shore
Him who gave the rings to them   in the times before
Lifeless on his bed of rest.   His ending-day had been
Unto him, the dauntless,   the Prince of Weder-kin,
Unto him, the Warrior-King,   a death of wondrous dying.
But erst had they espied there   a stranger creature lying—
The Serpent him beside there,   loathed for flame and flying.
That Drake, the grim and grisly,   was scorched by fire about;
Fifty foot he measured long,   all stretched out.
Aloft he'd had his joy of air   in night-times past,
And down again had gone to den.   In death now fast,
He would use his earthly lair   nevermore at last.
The jars and the goblets   were standing by him here,
And platters here were lying,   and good swords dear,
Rusted and eaten through,   even as of old
They'd houséd in earth's bosom   a thousand winters told.
This heritage had magic might: this by-gone mortals' gold
Had been by spells encircled,   that none of human kind
Could ever touch that treasure-hall,   save him whom God designed
(The Sooth-King of victories,   Helper, he, of men),
Whomsoe'er he deeméd fit   to open hoard and den.

Beowulf

XLII

THE *Scop chants how in truth Beowulf had been doomed to die because the treasure was under a fatal spell. (Yet he tells us that Beowulf was under God's protecting care; and it would seem that here, as in several places in his poem, he has mingled heathen and Christian ideas—as many people do still.) He chants next the speech of the faithful kinsman, Wiglaf, who now bethought him of the funeral pyre. And then Wiglaf went with seven chosen men and pillaged the Hoard of all that remained. And the warriors pushed the Monster's bulk over the cliff into the sea. And they laded a wagon with the treasure, and marched with the body of Beowulf to Whale's Ness.*

THEN 'twas plain to seeing   his quest had fared not well
Who under wall had plundered wealth,   within, against the spell
Erst had the Keeper slaughtered   someone of a few,
And so the feud avengéd   with horrible to-do.
A wonder 'tis the manner   a man may meet his end,
Even a famous jarlman,   when with kin and friend,
'Tis his within the mead-house   no longer now to dwell.
And thus with Beowulf it was: when he that Keeper sought
And that close encounter,   he himself knew naught
Of what should cause his parting   from the world away;
For the mighty chieftains   who there the treasure hid
Had spake a curse upon it till   earth's doomsday—
That whosoever robbed the floor   should be a man forbid,
Pent in demon-places,   in hell-bonds fast,
A sinner racked by plague-spots.   Yet Beowulf, he cast
His glances more on Heaven's grace   than gold unto the last.
   Wiglaf made a speech then,   son of Weohstan:
"Many a jarl must often,   for will of one man,
Suffer a great bitterness—   even now as we.
Nor might we rede our lief Lord,   Shepherd of the free,

Beowulf

Not to greet that Gold-Guard,   but to let him lie
Yonder where he long was   and dwell his cavern by,
Ever unto world's end.   But Beowulf, not he!—
Held he to his high fate.   The Hoard is ours to see,
Albeit grimly gotten.   Too strong the destiny
That thither lured our Folk-King.   I was in the hall,
And of that chambered treasure   had my look at all;
When by chance I'd found there,   none too pleasantly,
A pathway in and under   that earth-wall.
With hands I seized me swiftly,   from the treasure-store,
A burthen big and mickle;   and hither out I bore
Back unto my own King.   Quick as yet was he,
Wise, with wits about him,   and spake he full and free,
The Agéd in his anguish,   and sent farewells to ye,
And bade ye that ye build him,   for deeds of him, your Friend,
A barrow, a high one,   yonder on land's end,
Memorial, mickle barrow,   where his pyre shall be—
For worthiest warrior was he,   wide across the earth,
Whilst still he wielded burg-wealth,   of all of human birth.
Let us hasten yonder   to seek and see anew
Under wall the wonder—   the heap I'll show to you;
Where of rings and broad gold   anear enough ye'll view.
Be the bier ready,   ordered anon,
By our coming back here;   we will bear him on,
Our own Lord, our dear man,   to where for long and late
In the Wielder's shelter   he'll abide his fate."
    Then the Boy of Weohstan,   Hero battle-stout,
Bade order many warriors   of homesteads round about
Thither to fetch the bale-wood   from far for him, the Great,
Him, the people's Ruler: "Now shall fire devour,
As wax the murky flames now,   the fighters' Man-of-power,
Him who oft abided   of old the iron-shower,

When the storm of arrows,   speeded by the strings,
Shot above the shield-wall   swift on feathered wings,
And shaft fulfilled its duty   and drave the barb to goal."
   Of sooth, the son of Weohstan,   Wiglaf, wise of soul,
Chose from out the followers,   thane-men of the King's,
The seven best together,   and under roof of hate
Went he with the warriors,   himself as one of eight,
And one who walked ahead there   bare a torch in hand.
Nor was there any drawing-lots   among that eager band
For who that Hoard should pillage,   when they saw in hall
It resting reft of Keeper   and lost it lying all.
And little were they mourning,   as out they carried fast
The treasure-trove, the priceless.   The Dragon, eke they cast,
The Worm, over the wall-cliff,—   let the wave take,
Let the flood embosom   the Hoard-Ward Drake.
The aethelings they piled a wain   with twisted gold beyond a guess,
And bare the hoary Hero on,   up Whale's Ness.

XLIII

THE Scop *chants the funeral rites, how they built a pyre and hung it with war-gear and set on it the body of Beowulf, and how they all mourned about the flames. And with them his Wife. (The Scop has not mentioned his wife before —had Beowulf perhaps married Hygelac's widow, Hygd, who, it seems, had liked him?) Then the Geats raised, as Beowulf had bidden, a memorial mound on the*

Beowulf

adland, and they surrounded the place of the burning with a wall, and they
id away in the mound all the treasure that Beowulf thought he had won for his
eople's joy. And then,—last scene of all that ends this strange, eventful history
—twelve of the Geats rode around the mound singing their sorrow and their
raise. It must have been a beautiful and majestic ceremony. But is it not
range that Beowulf should have been honored with such purely pagan rites, and
hat no cross was set over the mound? Not really strange. For, in spite of all
he Scop says about the Christian's God, Beowulf and Hrothgar and Hygelac and
l of those bygone worthies were still little touched in their real feelings and
ustoms by the new doctrines and customs of the Christian missionaries and
onks; and the Scop, for all his wistful piety, was at heart something of a pagan
o. But Beowulf was a good man and great, for all that.

THEN for him the Geats made   the pyre, firm on earth,
And hung it with helmets,   with byrnies a-sheen,
And with battle-bucklers,   as his prayer had been.
And they laid amid it   the Prince of wondrous worth,
Laid their Lord belovéd,   weeping in their dearth.
And upon the hill-top   the warriors awoke
The mightiest of bale-fires.   Rose the wood-smoke,
Swart above the blazing.   And the roar of flame
Blended was with wailing,   as still the winds became,
Till, hot unto his heart, it broke   the Geat's bone-frame.
Unglad of mood, in grief they mourned   their great Chief dead.
And his Wife, with hair bound,   her song of sorrow said,
Over and over: how 't was hers to dread
Days of harm and hardship,   warriors' fall and grame,
The terror of the raider,   captivity and shame.
   The sky the reek had swallowed.   The Weders raised thereby
A mound upon the headland,   that was broad and high,
Seen afar from ocean   by sailors on their ways,
And built the battle-bold One   a beacon in ten days.

117

Beowulf

Around the brands and ashes   a wall they ran and wrought,
The worthiest contriving   of men of wisest thought.
And in the barrow set they   ring and gem and plate,
And all the splendor-booty   out of hoard of late
Forth their hands had taken,   urged by heads of hate.
They gave the wealth of jarlmen   to earth for to hold,
Now where yet it liveth,   in the mould, the gold,
As useless unto mortals   as it was of old.
   Then around the mound rode,   with cry and call,
Bairns of the aethelings,   twelve of all,
To mourn for their Master,   their sorrow to sing,
Framing a word-chant,   speaking of the King:
They vaunted his earlship,   they honored doughtily
His wonder-works of glory.   Let it ever be,
That heart of man shall cherish   and word of man shall praise
The Master-Friend, when in the end   his spirit goes its ways.
So the Geatish clansmen   bemoanéd their dearth,
The passing-forth of Beowulf,   these comrades of his hearth,
Calling him a World-King,   the mildest under crown,
And to his kin the kindest,   and keenest for renown.

Beowulf

THE FIGHT AT FINNSBURG

(A fragment of a lost ballad)

[A WATCHER cried to clansmen]:   "Our gables are aflame!"
And thus the King made answer,   the young in battle-fame:
"That glare is not the sunrise,   is not a dragon's flight,
Nor are aflame our gables   here on hall tonight.
But hither cometh, bearing . . . .
. . . .   Now sing the birds of prey,
And the wolf, the grey-coat,   howleth his cries;
Resoundeth the spear-wood,   shield to shaft replies.
Now is shining yonder,   under clouds, the moon;
Now are deeds arising,   to whelm my people soon.
But wake ye now, my warsmen,   lapped in linkéd mail,
Resolve, and rage ye vanward,   in mood that cannot quail."
    Then rose the golden clansmen,   and girt their swords amain;
Then hastened to the doorway   the noble heroes twain,
Eaha and Sigeferth,   and drew their blades before,
While Ordlaf and Guthlaf   sped to the other door,
Whom himself did Hengest   follow down the floor.
    Yet Guthere to Garulf   was pleading out there,
That he, a boy so high of birth,   his weapon should forbear
In the first encounter   at the doors of hall,
Lest Sigeferth, the veteran,   wrest it him withal.
But Garulf to the foeman   shouted boldly o'er,
Garulf, keen for contest: "Who is it holds the door?"
"My name," quoth he, "is Sigeferth—   prince of the Secgas, son!
A wanderer and warrior   in many a battle won.

Beowulf

Widely couth my war-work; and here awaiteth thee
Whatever fate that thou, boy, think'st to seek from me."
    Then was at the wall there din of slaughter-strife,
As broke the bosséd bucklers, the shields that shelter life,
In hands there of the hardy. Resounded floor of hall,
Till crumpled in the contest Garulf, best of all
Who dwelt in Frisian home-land,— son of Guthlaf, he—
And with him many a good man. Hovered waveringly
The raven, swart and sallow-brown, about above the dead,
And the light of battle-swords flashed so and spread,
It seemed as if on fire were all Finn's burg-stead.
I never heard that worthier e'er were men in war,
Nor sixty fierce defenders better fought before,
Nor liegemen better paid back ever the sweet mead
Than Hnaef's retainers Hnaef repaid by brave sword-deed.
    And five days they fought there, so well that of that corps
Never fell a man there; but still they held the door.
And then a wounded hero wended him away;
Said that now his byrnie was broken through,
His war-harness useless, his helmet piercéd too.
And then anon did ask him the Fender of the Folk,
How the bleeding warsmen were biding each stroke,
Or which now of the two braves ....

This special edition of "Beowulf" has been composed in Garamond types and printed in New York by the Duenewald Printing Corporation on rag paper especially made by the Worthy Paper Company. The illustrations are from drawings in line and water-color made for this edition by Lynd Ward.